Awful Ends

THE BRITISH MUSEUM
BOOK OF EPITAPHS

C. Grignion sculp.

Awful Ends

THE BRITISH MUSEUM BOOK OF EPITAPHS

David M. Wilson

BRITISH MUSEUM PRESS

To
Caygill, Chattington and Clear
They have put up with a lot

Published by British Museum Press
A division of
The British Museum Company Ltd
46 Bloomsbury Street,
London WC1B 3QQ

First published 1992
First published in paperback 1998

Designed by James Shurmer

Set in Linotype Joanna
by Rowland Phototypesetting Ltd,
Bury St Edmunds, Suffolk
and printed and bound in Great Britain
by The Bath Press Ltd, Avon.

A catalogue record
for this book is available from the
British Library.

ISBN 0 7141 1781 1

Frontispiece
The frontispiece to a 1753 edition
of Thomas Gray's
Elegy written in a Country Churchyard,
engraved by C. Grignion
from a design by R. Bentley.

CONTENTS

PREFACE

As an archaeologist I have been professionally involved with funerary inscriptions for more than forty years. I have naturally,therefore, taken an interest in epitaphs of later ages as I have walked round churchyards in pursuit of my narrower interests. In a period of my life when I was not able to get down to serious academic work I started to put together this little anthology for my own enjoyment and that of one or two friends who enjoy the more bizarre horizons of the epitaph writer. It has grown into something which has taken the form of a bedside book. I hope readers will get as much fun out of it as I got in compiling it. Many of the epitaphs recorded here will be familiar to the epitaph buff – but I hope that I may introduce even the specialist to some of the wider lunacies and pathos of funerary inscriptions written in the English language.

This work could not have been completed without a considerable amount of help and goodwill from friends and colleagues. John Curtis, Vivian Davies and Tim Potter taught me about the prehistory of epitaphs. Leslie Webster, Andrew Oddy and a host of others have contributed texts. Antony Griffiths and Hilary Williams have helped with the illustrations. The three ladies to whom this book is dedicated have supported me not only in this work, but in a vast amount of writing and publishing over the past fifteen years; to them go especial thanks.

The main secondary sources I have used are listed at the end of the book, and where I quote a source in the running text, I do so by the name of the author – whose work is then to be found in the List of Sources (which is not, I must insist, a bibliography of the whole vast subject).

All illustrations come from the British Museum except for that on page 94 which is courtesy of the British Library. Each chapter opens with designs from 18th-century funeral cards.

The following copyrights in the epitaphs are acknowledged with thanks: Chatto and Windus, from *Possession* by A. S. Byatt, p. 28; Faber and Faber Ltd, from *Collected Shorter Poems* by W. H. Auden, pp. 91–2; Mrs Basil Gray and the Society of Authors for the estate of Laurence Binyon, p. 59; *The New Statesman and Nation* and M. Fagg, p. 92; Peters, Fraser and Dunlop and the estate of J. B. Morton, p. 94; A. P. Watt and the estate of Robert Graves, p. 93.

(*Facing page*) *Bushey Churchyard* by William Henry Hunt. Hunt was a protégé of the collector and physician Dr Monro, who appears on horseback on the right. In the drawing are the tombs of two of Monro's other protégés and friends, Thomas Hearne and Henry Edridge, together with that of his son Henry Monro, a promising artist who died aged 23. Pen and ink with watercolour.

INTRODUCTION

The British Museum is a serious institution, one that sometimes seems to deal almost exclusively with death and destruction. Its vast collections comprise the funerary detritus of the whole world from pre-dynastic Egypt to the paper accompaniments of the modern Malaysian Chinese on their way to hell. The Museum has funerary inscriptions in all sorts of language, from Hindi to Hebrew, from Anglo-Saxon to Babylonian, and in all scripts from Greek to hieroglyphs and runes. It unfortunately has few if any English monumental inscriptions – few epitaphs. This seems to me a pity. It is for this reason that I have attempted to remedy a perceived defect in the Museum's collections. For among the most interesting of the remains of man are his funerary arrangements and the British have a vast wealth of these. To this extent the Museum is not typical, but as it has a cat book and a cook book, so it should have an epitaph book – a book for not too serious enjoyment. For, although the Museum is a serious institution, it should never take itself too seriously.

The book has certain deliberate limitations. I have in no way tried to discuss the history, typology or language of funerary inscriptions in any but the most superficial fashion. Apart from my introductory chapter I have included only one inscription in any other language but those that are native to the British Isles; this in spite of great temptation. Few, for example, could resist quoting one of the more splendid epitaphs in Père Lachaise cemetery in Paris:

Ici repose Colette.

I, however, have succeeded! All the inscriptions in this book are rendered in English; I have resorted to translation only in the few quotations of medieval inscriptions. Further, I have eschewed all consistency of punctuation, of capitalisation, of lineation and even, in some cases, of spelling – a blessed relief to an academic! I have also ignored the use of *y* for *th* wherever possible – let us leave the form 'ye' to tea-shoppes and the like or, in the subjective, to Quakers. I have also ignored all italicisation, a feature which amounted to an epidemic in the eighteenth century.

I have also avoided all mention of animals; but, so that my prejudices do not become too obvious, I must quote here the single most famous epitaph of the nineteenth century, by John Cam Hobhouse on Byron's dog:

> Beneath this stone are deposited the remains of one who possessed Beauty
> without Vanity, Strength without Insolence, Courage without Ferocity,
> and all the Virtues of Man without his Vices. This praise which would be
> unmeaning Flattery, if inscribed over human ashes, is but a just Tribute
> to the Memory of BOATSWAIN, a dog.

Byron himself fared much worse when he was finally buried at Hucknall Torkard.

A word as to sources. Many books have been dedicated to epitaphs, the earliest in the seventeenth century. Many serious treatises and articles have been published on the subject and many lists made. Anthologies abound and, in the words of one anthologist – Fritz Spiegl – 'anthologists have been merrily anthologizing each other for nearly two centuries . . . Nor were they always too concerned with accuracy of transcription; and most telling of all, it transpires that many of the most quoted epitaphs have never been on gravestones at all'. This simply adds to the pleasure of compilation. I have, however, tried to sort the known from the recorded and the recorded from the reputed – even the imagined from the invented. But this is a bedside book and I cannot vouch for the accuracy of every inscription, although many of them have been copied by my own hand in churches and cemeteries throughout the country. I have also copied epitaphs from the great series of parish histories which were such a feature of the leisured nineteenth century. Some come from public buildings and others even from that extraordinary modern phenomenon, the park bench. Where it seemed appropriate I have quoted sources; sometimes, however, vulgarly popular examples have been quoted with no such acknowledgement.

In writing this book I have always been conscious that epitaphs are written at a time of emotional stress. Although the British have a strong tradition of compiling and executing light-hearted, canting and convoluted inscriptions on tombs and memorials, some memorials are too moving to be recorded here. In one of my local parish churches, for example, is a wall plaque which records the death of two children – 'in each other's arms' – after having been ship-wrecked off the coast of Madagascar in the middle of the last century. The delicate wording of this inscription still has the power to affect one's senses; and who could fail to be moved by the small stone in the graveyard of the same church, which is simply, almost brutally, inscribed, 'Cholera 1832'? This book is not written in a mocking mode.

There is a strong tradition in this country of memorial writings which were not carved on tombstones or on wall plaques. Of particular importance are the occasional poems and epitaphs, written on paper and posted near a tomb – a practice familiar to the student of the sixteenth and seventeenth centuries. Thus Leonato in *Much Ado about Nothing*, 'Hang her an epitaph upon her tomb', refers to this custom, which is also frequently encountered in topographical works until quite late in the eighteenth century. Such, for example, was the famous couplet (part of a longer poem which may have originally been written in French) to Sir Philip Sidney posted in Old St Paul's Cathedral:

> *The Heavens have his Soule, the Arts his Fame,*
> *All Souldiers the Grief, the World his Good Name.*

Many of the inscriptions quoted here have been culled from secondary sources. The reason for this is that many of the inscriptions have vanished – worn out by the weather, obliterated by the feet of time, by the hammers of vandals or by the vandalism of planners. This country has not yet come to the unfortunate level of Denmark, where grave markers are discarded after ten years unless special permission has been granted to the deceased's family. This produces pathetic little stones with pathetic inscriptions and no date – 'mother' and no more. Pride in family and place of origin is lost. Even in this country parsons are often not the best custodians of their freehold, and governments care less for the monuments of the past unless it be monuments to parliamentary luminaries. So far there seem to be no EEC regulations concerning epitaphs, but we may expect them momentarily – take heed from the epitaph by a civil servant on p. 91! There is no doubt that there is a tendency in the twentieth century for ghastly good taste to take over our graveyards. There are nowadays few exciting memorials, fewer epitaphs; ecclesiastical authorities chivvy and arbiters of good taste indulge in italic scripts faultlessly spaced, a feature which is beginning to ruin Westminster Abbey's long and eccentric tradition of memorial inscriptions.

We are losing a whole aspect of our culture as regulations defeat the efforts of the imaginative – few people alive today have seen a weeping angel or a broken column erected over the grave of someone they knew. The complaints of modern arbiters of taste echo familiarly down the centuries; in 1631 Weever was complaining like a modern guitar-playing dean that:

> They garnish their Tombes, now adayes, with the pictures of naked men and women; raising out of the dust and bringing unto the Church, the memories of the heathen gods and goddesses, with all their whirligiggs: and this (as I take it) is most the fault of the Tombemakers, than theirs who set them aworke . . .'

Weever, however, was well attuned to the importance of epitaphs, composing a poem which might well serve as a challenge to the archaeologists of the British Museum:

> If you esteeme not these as things above the ground,
> Looke under, where the urnes of ancient times are found:
> The Roman Emprours Coynes, oft digd out of the dust,
> And warlike weapons, now consum'd with cankring rust,
> And huge and massy bones of mighty fearfull men,
> To tell the worlds full strength, what creatures lived then,
> When in her height of youth, the lustie fruitfull earth
> Brought forth her big-lim'd brood, even Gyants in their birth.

Weever himself was given the epitaph he deserved (p. 78).

Many of the great and good have written about epitaphs, mostly in terms that are ineffably boring or pious. I would not recommend anybody to read William Wordsworth on the subject, although he approved of Milton's epitaph on Shakespeare (p. 25). Dr Johnson delivered himself in *The Gentleman's Magazine* of a typical verbose and patronising essay (so verbose indeed that my editor has refused to let me quote more than the bare minimum):

> Tho' a sepulchral Inscription is professedly a Panegyric, and, therefore, not confined to historical Impartiality, yet it ought always to be written with regard to the Truth. No man ought to be commended for *Virtues* which he never possessed, but whoever is curious to know his Faults must enquire after them in other Places . . .

> The best Subject for EPITAPHS is private Virtue; Virtue exerted in the same Circumstances in which the Bulk of Mankind are placed, and which, therefore, may admit of many Imitators. He who has delivered his

Country from Oppression, or freed the World from Ignorance or Error,
can excite the Emulation of a very small Number; but he that has repell'd
the Temptations of Poverty, and disdained to free himself from Distress at
the Expence of his Virtue, may animate Multitudes by his example . . .

Which is nonsense, as witness Dr Johnson's own composition of an epitaph for Oliver Goldsmith, which being in Latin must escape this book. This got him into terrible trouble from many of his friends, including Edmund Burke, Joshua Reynolds and R. B. Sheridan. Burke composed a round-robin of protest asking for the epitaph to be rendered in English; it starts splendidly:

. . . the monument for Dr Goldsmith, which considered abstractedly,
appears to be, for elegant composition and masterly style, in every respect
worthy of the pen of the learned author . . . [we] are yet of the opinion
that the character of the deceased as a writer, particularly as a poet, is
perhaps not delineated with all the exactness which Dr Johnson is capable
of giving it . . .

Ironically Johnson's epitaph to Goldsmith was destroyed during the bombing of the Temple Church in London during the Second World War and all that survives is a coped tombstone against a wall of the churchyard with the simple inscription 'Goldsmith'.

Many of these essayists spend some time stressing the obvious: that the sentiments expressed in the immediacy of death do not reflect what the memorialist feels in the fullness of time – as witness the story of the Madden inscriptions spelt out at some length below (p. 20f.). Epitaphs are generally unreliable historical documents. Sometimes they reflect true sentiments; sometimes the sentiments are in fact other persons' flowers; sometimes of course they dress up in purple and fine linen the blue jeans of everyday life. This point has been made often and eloquently, as for example by Crabbe:

. . . Let not love nor grief believe
That we assent – who neither loved nor grieve –
To all that praise which on the tomb is read,
To all that passion dictates for the dead;
But more indignant we the tomb deride,
Whose bold inscription flattery sells to pride.

There is no reason to belabour this point; epitaphs can be read at all levels and enjoyed at all levels, from piety to cynicism. Samuel Wesley wrote concerning a monument to Samuel Butler erected in Westminster Abbey forty-one years after his death:

While Butler (needy wretch!) was yet alive,
No gen'rous patron would a dinner give:
See him, when starv'd to death and turn'd to dust,
Presented with a monumental bust!
The poet's fate is here in emblem shown,
He ask'd for bread, and he received a stone.

Epitaphs have many uses. They have been much consulted by genealogists – amateur and professional alike – and have in many local studies been used for demographic purposes. They have not to my knowledge been used in place-name studies, although they might in particular be of use in the study of minor names – farms and the like: they also produce some useful spellings. Although sometimes appearing in general anthologies, they are in many respects a neglected element in the study of literature. They have certainly been much neglected by historians of the English language, who, having used tons of paper examining Old English inscriptions, have rarely allowed more than a footnote to monumental occurrences of words or constructions of a later date. Words like *landladie* (at Woolland, Dorset) and *virginall* – the instrument not the condition – (in Norwich Cathedral) occur in very early contexts and could well be used with many other lapidary terms in PhD theses. They might well have a use in the study of dialects, as in the study of punctuation. (Punctuation in English inscriptions even in the present day is eccentric in the extreme.) Here epitaphs are collected for entertainment – a most worthy aim!

I have taken pleasure in including in this small collection some epitaphs written epigrammatically concerning those who are not dead, or have not lived. Those well versed in this genre will notice that I have not given a provenance to one epitaph much beloved by collectors of casual verse (it is said by some to be American. Kingsley Amis is more honest and – attributing it to Peterborough Cathedral – says he found it in an undated nineteenth-century book of epitaphs):

Reader, pass on! – don't waste your time
On bad biography and bitter rhyme.
For what I am this cumbrous clay insures
And what I was, is no affair of yours.

I

IN MEMORIAM

The first memorial inscriptions in the British Isles are of Roman date (first to fifth centuries AD); here is one from South Shields. I wonder what this Levantine made of the frozen north and of his northern wife?

> *To the Gods of the lower regions: Regina, freedwoman and wife of*
> *Barates of Palmyra, a Catuvellaunian by tribe.*

There is a tenuous continuity of Roman epigraphic tradition in the Celtic west after the Romans had left these islands. Many inscriptions are quite simple in sentiment, recording merely the name of the person commemorated. The most splendid Welsh epitaph of the early medieval period concerns the family which ruled Powys from the seventh to ninth centuries. Only part of the ninth-century inscription on this pillar has been deciphered. Translated from the Latin it boasts, in normal Welsh fashion, about a victory over the English; here is the most coherent passage:

> *. . . Concenn, therefore, being great-grandson of Eliseg, erected this stone*
> *to his great-grandfather Eliseg. It is Eliseg who annexed the inheritance of*
> *Powys . . . through nine years (took it) from the power of the English*
> *with sword and with fire. Whosoever shall read this hand-inscribed stone,*
> *let him give a blessing on the soul of Eliseg.*

Valle Crucis Abbey, Denbighshire

The earliest English inscriptions (where they survive) are very simple, bearing either a name or a short formula, for example, 'Pray for the soul of . . .'. Thus at Hartlepool, Co. Durham (now in the Museum of Antiquities at Newcastle upon Tyne), a carved stone slab of late seventh- or eighth-century date bears an inscription in Latin:

> *Pray for Vermund [and] Torhtsuid.*

The first name is a man's, the second a woman's; not very exciting, but one of the first full English epitaphs to have survived. A little later in date is the very grand decorated stone at Ruthwell, Dumfriesshire, which bears Latin and Old English inscriptions, in both Latin and runic characters. This may have been a memorial stone, but if so the epitaph does not survive, although a fragment of one of the most moving poems in the English language, *The Dream of The Rood*, is included among the texts inscribed on it.

Two or three inscriptions will suffice to give a taste of pre-Conquest epitaphs, the first in Latin dated to the early eighth century:

> *Here in the tomb rests Herebericht the priest in the body.*
>
> Monkwearmouth parish church, Co. Durham

An eleventh-century stone from Berkshire records the (Norse) name of the writer of the Latin inscription:

> *On 24 September Ægelward son of Kypping was put in this place. Blessed be the man who prays for his soul. Toki wrote me.*
>
> Stratfield Mortimer

The Scandinavians were much more prone to advertise their skill as craftsmen. A splendidly carved, tenth-century stone at Kirk Michael in the Isle of Man has a runic Norse inscription, which concludes with a proud piece of self advertisement:

> *Mailbrikti, son of Athakan the smith, raised this cross for his soul and that of his brother. Gautr made this and all in Man.*

At home the Vikings sometimes took a rather mercenary view of a dead man – with no sense of criticism of course. A group of runic stones set up in Sweden in the 1020s records the memory of Ulv of Borresta:

> *And Ulv took three gelds in England. That was the first that Toste paid. Then Thorkel paid. Then Canute paid.*
>
> Yttergärde, Uppland, Sweden

From the centuries after the Norman Conquest, more funerary inscriptions have survived. Few epitaphs in the English language survive, however, until the sixteenth century. Ravenshaw claims – and who would deny him – that the earliest epitaph in English is that dated 1370 at Brightwell-Baldwin, Oxfordshire:

> Man come & se how schal alle dede be: we you comes bad and bare:
> Noth hab ven be away fare: all ys werines yt ve for care
> But yt ve do for godys luf we have nothyng yare: Hundyr
> Yis grave lys John ye Smith. God gif hys soule heven grit.

The Norman French inscription on the tomb of the Black Prince (died 1376) in Canterbury Cathedral is important as a model for one of the commonest of all English inscriptions. It is here given in an old translation, quoted by Pettigrew and slightly altered:

> Whoso thou be that passeth by,
> Where these corpses interred lie:
> Understand what I shall say,
> As at this time speak I may.
> Such as thou art, sometime was I;
> Such as I am, so shall you be.
> I little thought on the hour of death,
> So long as I enjoyed breath;
> Greate riches here I did possess,
> Wherof I made great nobleness;
> I had gold, silver, wardrobe and
> Great treasures, horses, houses, land,
> But now a catiff poor am I,
> Deep in the ground, lo here I lie!
> My beauty great is all quite gone,
> My flesh is wasted to the bone,
> My house is narrow now and throng
> Nothing but truth comes from my tongue:
> And if you should see me this day,
> I do not think but you would say,
> That I had never been a man;
> So much altered now I am!
>
> For God's sake pray to heaven's king
> That he my soul to heaven would bring;
> All they that pray and make accord
> For me unto my God and Lord;

God place them in his paradise
Wherin no wretched catiff lies.

The first six lines of this verse have an origin lost in antiquity, but they have been repeated in various forms on tombstones throughout the British Isles. Here are two examples which differ greatly in date; the first of the early seventeenth century:

All you that do this place pass bye
Remember death for you must dye
As you are now even so was I
And as I am so shall you be.

Thomas Gooding here do staye
Wayting for God's judgement daye

Norwich Cathedral

On the other side of the British Isles in Kirk Braddan, in the Isle of Man, is a much later stone, perhaps more artlessly scanned, but expressing a similar sentiment:

John Creer of Renscault
departed this life March 20th 1791 aged 67 years.
Scoff not at me as you pass by
For as now you are so once was I.
Altho my body is turn'd to dust
I hope to rise amongst the just.

THE DEAR DEPARTED

From the sixteenth century onwards British epitaphs are often fulsome, cloy-
ing, sentimental or worse. Fortunately many of them express these sentiments
in the Latin language, which I have ruled out of court in this book. Some use
both Latin and English, such as the memorial of John Green of Ensham, who
died aged twenty-eight in 1632. The Latin text encloses this verse:

> Stay reader drop upon this stone
> One pitying tear and then be gone.
> A handsome pyle of flesh and blood
> Is here sunk down to its first mud,
> Which thus in Western rubbish lyes
> Until the Eastern Starr shall rise.

More dignified certainly is this:

> Sacred
> To the memory of Mr Fermor Pepys
> sometimes of this parish.
> Of a worthy, Decent,
> most happy nature,
> good education &c.,
> tried faith to God,
> a persecuted church,
> a banisht prince,

& his old friend.
Obijt Sept. 12. 1660.
Ætat 79.

Mileham, Norfolk

The seventeenth century produced some rather good epitaphs in this vein –
witness the memorial to Sir Robert Shirley who died for his royalist convictions
in the Tower of London during the Civil War:

Whose singular praise it is
to have done the best thinges in the worst of times
And
hoped them in the most callamitous.

Staunton Harold, Leicestershire

In the church of St Denis at Colmworth, Bedfordshire, is the splendid alabaster tomb erected in 1641 by Catherine Dyer in memory of her husband, Sir
William. The grandeur of the tomb barely overshadows the moving verse:

My dearest dust, could not thy hasty day
Afford thy drowszy patience leave to stay
One hower longer: so that we might either
Sate up, or gone to bedd together?
But since thy finisht labour hath possest
Thy weary limbs with early rest,
Enjoy it sweetly: and thy widdowe bride
Shall soone repose her by thy slumbring side.
Whose business, now, is only to prepare
My nightly dress, and call to prayre:
My eyes wax heavy and the day growes old.
The dew falls thick, my belovd grows cold.
Draw, draw the closed curtaynes: and make roome:
My dear, my dearest dust; I come, I come.

Ravenshaw quotes an epitaph from Easingwold, Yorkshire, commemorating a
woman I am sorry not to have met:

S. M. Anne Harrison, well known by the name of NANNA RAN DAN,
who was chaste, but no prude; & tho' free yet no harlot. By Principle
vertuous, by Education a Protestant; her freedom made her liable to
censure, while her extensive charities made her esteemed. Her tongue she
was unable to control, but the rest of her members she kept in subjection.
After a life of 80 years thus spent, she died 1745.

The following epitaph, typical of its period and of the century and a half which succeeded it, is worth quoting almost in its entirety. I have, for the sake of sense and my own reason, punctuated it to taste, and have ignored all capital letters and line endings:

> *Mary Relict of Kildare, Ld Digby.*
> *Departed this life Decembr.*
> *23 An.Dom. 1692*
> *Whom it were unpardonable to lay down in silence and of whom it is difficult to speak with justice. For her just character will look like flattery and the least abatement of this injury to her memory. In every condition of life she was a pattern to her sex, appeared mistress of those peculiar qualities that were requisite to conduct her through it with honour, and never failed to exert them in their proper seasons with the utmost advantage. She was modest without affectation, easy without levity and reserved without pride; knew how to stoop without sinking and to gain people's affections without lessening their regards. She was careful without anxiety, frugal without parsimony; not at all fond of the superfluous trappings of greatness, yet abridged herself in nothing that her quality required. She was a faithful member of the Church of England, her piety was exemplary, her charity universal. She found herself a widow at the beginning of her life when the temptations of beauty, honour, youth, and pleasure were in their full strength; yet she made them all give way to the interest of her family and betook herself entirely of the matron's part . . . In a word she was truly wise, truly honourable, and truly good. More can scarce be said, and yet he that says this knew her well and is well assured he has said nothing which either veracity or modesty should oblige him to suppress.*

Coleshill, Warwickshire

Stone monuments are fairly hardy objects and the fear of literal mistakes must often worry mason and patron alike. Sometimes even the most sophisticated get the quotation wrong on a memorial. In 1991 *The Observer* pointed out that a new memorial to Thomas Paine at the Angel, Islington, London, had (as well as a missing comma in one passage) misquoted both *The Age of Reason* and *The Rights of Man*. The passage from *The Rights of Man* should read:

> *My country is the world and my religion is to do good.*

It appears, however, as:

> *My country is my world and my religion is to do good.*

which is quite a shift in meaning.

Correction is, however, rather more common than might be thought. When the wife of a keeper in the British Museum died in childbirth in 1830 her husband recorded his grief in his diary, together with two drafts of a deeply moving inscription, which becomes even more so when taken in its diary context. The inscription he chose is as follows:

Sacred to the memory of
Mary
The lovely and beloved wife of
Frederic Madden Esqre.
of the British Museum,
and daughter of Robert Hayton Esqre.
of Sunderland in the County of Durham
Born June 7th 1803.
After an inviolable attachment of ten years duration
unshaken by the united obstacles of fortune and prejudice
she was married in this church April 18th 1829,
and when ten short months had passed away in the enjoyment
of all that youth and beauty can bestow, and in the
anticipation of every happiness a fond heart can throb for,
to the inexpressible grief and horror of all who loved her
she expired on the 26th of February 1830,
having previously given birth the 21st inst. to an infant son
Frederick Hayton,
who survived his lamented mother only five days,
and lies by her side in the vaults beneath.
In remembrance of
her loveliness affection and virtue
her afflicted husband erects this monument
as the only means now left in his power
of testifying his lasting sorrow and regrets
She who was
To me the light, the breath of life is gone!
And memory now is as the faded flower
Whose lingering fragrance just recalls how sweet,
How beautiful it has been!

The first draft finished in a completely mawkish fashion with a verse which probably came from a *vade mecum* of epitaphs, for it is also recorded, by that totally unreliable source Susan Darling Stafford, in a nineteenth-century context at Newhaven, Connecticut:

> Early, bright, transient, chaste, as morning dew,
> She sparkled, was exhaled, and went to heaven.
> Poor dear lovely Mary!

Without underestimating the love and sorrow of Madden, this must surely rank high as one of the more excruciating sentiments ever to be proposed for a memorial, and it says a great deal for the good sense of the medievalist that he stopped it in time.

In this case we are fortunate in having a detailed description of the process which led to the erection of the monument. It was delivered to the church, St George's, Bloomsbury, on 25 August and fixed the following day. 'Where I wished to place it at first' – he writes – 'would have been a fee of 80 guineas, more than the cost of the Marble itself! I therefore changed my original

Sir Frederic Madden by W. Drummond.

21

intentions, and have now had it placed in a better situation for a fee of 20 guineas. My poor darling Mary!'

Madden remarried in 1837, but did not go back into the church until 1841 – this time for the christening of his son. In November 1862 the rather aged Sir Frederick Madden (note the added k to his Christian name) wrote in his diary, 'I caused the inscription on the Monument (written under circumstances of great distress and excitement) placed on it in 1830 to be erased, and another substituted in its place'. The memorial is in the east transept of St George's:

Sacred to the memory of
Mary
the beloved wife of

Frederick Madden Esqre
of the British Museum
and daughter of Robert Hayton Esqre
of Sunderland in the County of Durham
Born June 7th 1803
Married 18th April 1829
Died 26th February 1830
after giving birth to an infant son

Frederick Hayton
who survived only five days and lies
with his deeply lamented mother
in the vaults beneath

The sentimental verse is replaced by a Greek inscription, for which there is no known source; it may be translated, 'Alas! Alas! Wherefore did Hades/snatch away, snatch away from me my beloved child'.

The eighteenth century was sentimental in a rather different way, although a sister's love clearly differs from that of a doubly bereaved husband and father:

Erected by a sister in memory of her beloved Anna Cecilia, Daughter of Christopher Rhodes Esq; of Chatham in the County of Kent. She departed this Life, June 2d. 1796, aged 32. Her remains were deposited in the 42d vault in this Chapel. Distinguished by a fine Understanding, and a most amiable Disposition of Heart, She was the Delight of her Parents, and the Admiration of all who knew her. At the Age of 17, the small-pox stripped off all the Bloom of youthful Beauty, And being followed by a dreadful Nervous-disorder, withered those Prospects of earthly Happiness which were expected from her uncommon Affection, Sensibility and Tenderness. After suffering this afflictive Dispensation for many Years, when it was difficult to say which exceeded, her Sufferings or her

Submission; Her Friends concern for her Sorrows, or their Admiration of her Patience; She was released by Death, and received into that World where there shall be no more Pain, But GOD himself shall wipe away tears from every eye.

> Alas! how vain are feeble words to tell
> What once she was, and why I loved so well:
> None else but he who form'd the Heart can know
> How great her worth, or how extreme my woe!
> Blest Calv'ry, on the crimson Top I see,
> Suff'rings and Death with Life and Love agree;
> Justice severe and smiling Mercy join,
> And thro' the Gloom we see the Glory shine.

St James, Hampstead Road, London
(now demolished); the memorial is now in the Victoria and Albert Museum.

But not everybody was equally sentimental at this period. Ravenshaw quotes the following, two-edged, inscription from Lowestoft:

> In memory of
> Charles Ward
> who died May 1770
> Aged 63 years
> A dutiful son, a loving brother,
> and an affectionate husband.

> N.B. This stone was not erected by Susan his wife. She erected a stone to John Salter her second husband, forgetting the affection of Charles Ward her first Husband.

> Let no one disturb his bones.

In 1791 John Bowden of Chester saw that he might be on to a good thing. He published a book entitled *The Epitaph-Writer; consisting of six hundred original epitaphs, moral, admonitory, humorous and satirical . . . Chiefly designed for those who wish to write or engrave inscriptions on tombstones.* The title says it all and some of his more sugary effusions appeared as, to use his own words, 'Epitaphs for the middle and lower Ranks of People'. He had a high opinion of his own ability in this medium, but the reader must decide whether his judgement was sound:

> Here lies a Father, who on Earth
> Was neither rich nor great;
> Yet what he left, surpass'd in worth
> A Nobleman's Estate.

> To all who knew him it was giv'n,
> And is a Fortune ample;
> Better than House or Land (thank Heav'n)
> It was a good Example.

It is unclear whether he felt that ex-whores would own up on their tombstones, but this epitaph was designed 'for the tomb of a penitent prostitute':

> By Nature prone to ev'ry Vice,
> To Mis'ry swift to run;
> When Sinners did my Soul entice,
> I sinn'd – and was undone;
>
> But heav'nly Mercy, great and free,
> At length of Sin took place,
> And I became (what you may be)
> A Monument of Grace.

Fritz Spiegl has pointed out that this is not far away from the familiar verses that appear in the 'Deaths' columns of present-day local newspapers, of which he provides a seriously convoluted example:

> Evans, W. H. In memory of our beloved Dad.
>   My Heart is like a cabbage,
>   A cabbage cut in two,
>   The leaves are all that I have left
>   For my heart died with you.
> Your loving daughter Ena and son Ern.

Bowden's satirical lines are rather better than his sugary ones:

> Here lies a lewd Fellow, who, while he drew Breath,
> In the Midst of his Life was in Quest of his Death;
> Which he quickly obtain'd for it cost him his Life,
> For being in Bed with another Man's Wife.

Bowden was not the only one to produce books of epitaphs for the use of stonemasons, parsons or undertakers. Joseph Snow, in 1847, produced a book called *Lyra Memorialis. Original epitaphs and Churchyard thoughts in verse*, which was, said a review in *The Theologian*, 'in truth, a treasury of feeling, and we find in its simplicity its highest merit . . . to the clergy this volume may be of signal use.' The best epitaph in the book – and that is not saying much – is the only one not written by Snow; it is a verse written by John Milton in 1630:

What needs my Shakespeare for his honoured bones
The labour of an age in piled stones,
Or that his hallowed reliques should be hid
Under a star-ypointing pyramid?
Dear Son of Memory, great Heir of Fame,
What need'st thou such weak witness of thy Name?
Thou in our wonder and astonishment
Hast built thyself a livelong monument
And so sepulchred, in such pomp dost lie,
That kings for such a tomb would die.

From a very early period epitaphs were often used more to express the cleverness of the writer than the virtues of the departed. All sorts of twists and turns, including acrostics and anagrams, are found on tombstones. A slab in Lyme Regis Parish Church has a lengthy Latin inscription dating to 1636, which suddenly breaks into English:

Elisabeth Rose
Anag.
Oh blest arise.
Oh blest in faith, in life, in death,
In husband and posterytye
Arise to everlastynge joye
And blessed immortalitie

A funeral card etched by Francesco Bartolozzi after Edward Francis Burney in 1792. The veiled mourning figure is Genius, who is offered comfort by Fame. This design was used for the funeral card of Sir Joshua Reynolds in 1792.

Acrostics are popular on funerary inscriptions of all dates; they are particularly common in the sixteenth and seventeenth centuries. Many of them are banal, some exceedingly clever. I offer an example attributed to Ben Jonson, written for Margaret Ratcliffe:

M arble weepe, for thou dost cover
A dead Beautie undeneath thee,
R ich as Nature could bequeath thee;
G rant that no rude Hand remove her:
A ll the gazers on the skies
R ead not in fair Heav'ns Storie,
E xpresser Truth, or truer Glorie,
T han thy might in her bright Eyes.

R are as Wonder was her Wit,
A nd like Nectar, ever flowing;
T ill Time, strong by her bestowing,
C onquered hath both life and it:
L ife whose griefe was out of Fashion,
I n these Times. Few so have rued
F ate in a Brother. To conclude,
F or Wit, Feature, and true Passion,
E arth, thou hast not such another.

There is a certain opportunism in this epitaph from St Mary, Lambeth, which is worthy of the great Bowden himself:

Near to this place are the remains of
William Bacon
Of the Salt Office, London, gent.
Who was killed by thunder and lightning
at his window, July 12, 1787
Age 34 years.
By touch ethereal in a moment slain,
He felt the power of death, but not the pain;
Swift as the lightning glanced, his spirit flew,
And bade the rough tempestuous world adieu.
Short was his passage to that peaceful shore,
Where storms annoy and dangers threat no more.

Lightning strikes are often recorded on tombstones and sometimes most felicitously memorialised. This inscription at Stanton Harcourt, Oxfordshire, has a verse allegedly composed by Pope (another verse written jointly by Gay and Pope had been rejected by Lord Harcourt, who was paying for the stone):

Near this place lie the bodies of John Hewet and Sarah Drew, an industrious young man and virtuous maiden of this parish Contracted in Marriage who being with many others at Harvest work were both in one instant killed by lightning on the last day of July 1718.

> Think not by rigorous judgement seiz'd
> A pair so faithful could expire
> Victims so pure Heav'n saw well pleas'd
> And snatch'd them in coelestial fire
> Live well & fear no sudden fate
> When God calls virtue to the grave
> Alike 'tis Justice soon or late
> Mercy alike to kill or save.
> Virtue Unmov'd can hear the Call
> And face the flash that melts the Ball.

Frankness sometimes will out. The following epitaph is monstrously long, but is worth quoting in full, as every line seems to carry a new surprise:

> Beneath the remains of her Brother Edward
> And of her Husband Arthur
> Here lies the Body of Bridgett Applethwait
> Once Bridgett Nelson.
> After the Fatigues of a Married Life,
> Born by her with Incredible Patience,
> For four years and three Quarter, bating three weeks;
> And after the Enjoiment of the Glorious Freedom
> Of an Easy and Unblemisht Widowhood
> For four years and upwards,
> She Resolved to run the Risk of a Second Marriage-Bed
> But Death forbad the Banns
> And having with an *Apoplectic Dart*,
> (The same Instrument, with which he had Formerly
> Dispatch't her Mother)
> Touch't the most Vital part of her Brain;
> She must have fallen Directly to the Ground
> (as one Thunder-strook)
> If she had not been Catch'd and Supported
> by her intended Husband,
> Of which Invisible Bruise,
> After a long struggle of some Sixty Hours,
> With that Grand Enemy to Life,

(But the certain and Merciful Friend to
Helpless Old *Age*)
In Terrible Convulsion, Plaintive Groans
Or Stupefying Sleep
Without Recovery of her Speech or Senses,
She dyed on the 12th day of Sept in the Year
Of our Lord 1737 and of her own *Age* 44.
Behold I come as a Thief, Rev. 16th Ch: 15th v
But Oh! Thou Source of Pious Cares
Strict Judge without Regard
Grant, tho' we go hence Unawares
We go not Unprepar'd.
AMEN

Bramfield, Suffolk

By Victorian times such pleasantries were rather more rotundly expressed by the gentry. In her Booker Prize novel A. S. Byatt provides a splendid fictional epitaph of a Victorian lady:

Here lie the mortal remains of
Christabel Madeleine LaMotte
Elder daughter of Isidore LaMotte
Historian
And of his beloved wife
Arabel LaMotte
Only sister of Sophie, Lady Bailey
Wife of Sir George Bailey of Seal Court
Croysant le Wold

Born January 3rd 1825
Laid to rest May 8th 1890

After mortal trouble
Let me lie still
Where the wind drives and the clouds stream
Over the hill
Where grass's thousand thirsty mouths
Sup up their fill
Of the slow dew and the sharp rain
Of the mantling snow dissolv'd again
At Heaven's sweet will.

A. S. Byatt, *Possession: A Romance*, 1991.

This must be one of the few convincing nineteenth-century epitaphs to be written by a twentieth-century novelist. Perhaps, however, at the end one appreciates simplicity:

Elizabeth Noke Jan. 11. 1658
Duty while a child, love and care when a wife;
Courtesy and charity and a harmless life,
True piety to God: this shining seaven
Thro Jesus meritts took her soule to heaven.

Chicheley, Buckinghamshire

This sort of thing gets rather sickly in the nineteenth century, as witness the inscription on the tomb of Charlotte Lucy Beatrix Egerton, who died in 1845. Richard Westmacott, the sculptor of the deeply enigmatic pediment of the British Museum, carved a vision of the lady, asleep and watched over by a kneeling, rather self-satisfied angel in Rostherne Parish Church, Cheshire. On the tomb chest is carved:

Softly she slept – in the last hour
God's angel hover'd nigh;
He raised with love that fragile flower
To wake in bliss on high.

This aristocratic sentimentality survives into the twentieth century:

Mary Victoria
Lady Curzon of Keddleston
Born May 27 1870 died July 18 1906
Perfect in Love and Loveliness
Beauty was the least of her rare gifts
God had endowed with like graces
Her mind and soul
From illness almost unto death
Restored only to die
She was mourned in three continents
and by her dearest
will be
for ever unforgotten

Keddleston, Derbyshire

Most of the epitaphs listed so far in this section have recorded the virtues of women. Men are more rarely extolled with the same sincerity; this example is both exceptional and moving:

SAMUEL ALLY
An African and native of St Helena
Died the 28th of May 1822 aged 18 years
Born a slave and exposed
In early life to the corrupt influence
Of that unhappy state, he became
A model of TRUTH and PROBITY, for
The more fortunate of any country
or condition
This stone is erected by a grateful
Master, to the memory of a faithful
Servant, who repaid the boon of
Liberty with unbounded attachment

Kirk Braddan, Isle of Man

Servants are often remembered by their masters; a brass in Wing parish church, Buckinghamshire:

Honest old Thomas Cotes, that sometime was
Porter at Ascott-hall, hath now (alas)
Left his key, lodg, fyre, friends and all to have
a roome in heaven, this is that good man's grave.
Reader, prepare for thine, for none can tell
But that you two may meete to night, farewell
He dyed 20th of   Set up at the apoyntment
November 1648   and Charges of his friend
Geo: Houghton

One of the more informal statues in England – the subject seated, in wrinkled socks with dangling slipper – crowns the pedestal on which is recorded the epitaph of the man who gave his name to the future Prime Minister, William Ewart Gladstone. He looks rather nicer than the inscription suggests.

To the memory
of
William Ewart
An intelligent, indefatigable
and successful
merchant

A virtuous and amiable
man.
His widow and children
with the deepest feeling
of reverence and regret
have raised this monument
Born Feb. 26th 1763 – Died Oct. 4th l823

Liverpool, St James's Cemetery

Some epitaphs are merely puzzling; a plaque in the Old College building of Edinburgh University reads:

Sir Cowasji Jehangir Kt, CSI
The Peabody of the East

Why he is commemorated in Edinburgh is unclear; he was a Bombay philanthropist, particularly famous for his charitable donations to museums and hospitals. George Peabody (1795–1869), the American philanthropist, was famous in Britain for the 'Peabody Buildings', which provided working-class housing in London. (Peabody incidentally spent about a month after his death in Westminster Abbey – from 12 November to 11 December 1869 – before his body was removed to Massachusetts; a fact strangely recorded on the floor of the nave of Westminster Abbey – not far from the tomb of the Unknown Warrior. The use of Westminster Abbey as a temporary parking place for corpses can be noticed occasionally. Thus, for example, John, First Duke of Marlborough, was deposited in Westminster Abbey after his death in 1722; it was only in 1744 on the death of his duchess, Sarah, that his body was moved with hers to Blenheim.)

Scotland is a splendid place for epitaphs; the strict formality of that country's necropolises lends itself to pomposity, perhaps seen most strikingly in a comment on the tomb of one of the greatest figures of the Scottish Enlightenment, the philosopher David Hume, who died in 1776:

Within this circular idea
Called vulgarly a tomb,
The ideas and impressions lie
That constituted Hume.

On the circular shell of the actual tomb, on Calton Hill in Edinburgh, is, however, a brief Latin inscription and a record of Hume's birth and death days.

III

THE RUDE FOREFATHERS

The local churchyard provides us with some of the very best epitaphs. Scotland as always leads the way. Formality is totally dismissed in some of the most legendary of Scottish epitaphs, the best known of which allegedly comes from Aberdeen:

> *Here lie I, Martin Elginbrod.*
> *Have mercy on my soul, Lord God.*
> *As I on you, were I Lord God*
> *And you were Martin Elginbrod.*

Or, even more unlikely:

> *Here lie the bones of Elizabeth Charlotte,*
> *Born a virgin, died a harlot.*
> *She was aye a virgin at seventeen*
> *A remarkable thing in Aberdeen.*

But as the national poet, Robert Burns, spent a lot of his time slagging off the local village worthies, one might expect little else of Scotland. Here, for example, is Burns on James Humphrey, a mason of Mauchline (in the politer editions of his poetry it is entitled 'Epitaph on a noisy polemic'):

> *Below thir stanes lie Jamie's banes*
> *O Death, it's my opinion*
> *Thou ne'er took such a bleth'rin bitch*
> *Into thy dark dominion.*

Burns's most splendid epitaph is that of a schoolmaster of Cleish in Kinross:

> *Here lie Willie Michie's banes;*
> *O Satan, when ye tak him,*
> *Gie him the schoolin' of your weens,*
> *For clever deils he'll mak them.*

A surviving memorial in the Canongate Churchyard in Edinburgh shows another side of Burns:

> *Here lies*
> ROBERT FERGUSON POET
> *Born September 5th 1751*
> *Died October 16th 1774*
> *No sculptured Marble here nor pompous lay*
> *No storied urn nor animated Bust*
> *This simple Stone directs Pale Scotia's way*
> *To pour her Sorrows o'er her Poet's Dust*

On the back of the stone is a further inscription:

> *By Special grant of the Managers to Robert Burns who erected this Stone,*
> *this Burial place is to remain for ever Sacred to the memory of* ROBERT
> FERGUSON

Burns acknowledged his great debt to Ferguson and, visiting the grave in 1789, was shocked by its condition. He, therefore, after a ferocious correspondence with the kirk authorities, ordered the stone. It took two years to execute and two more before it was paid for. The stonemason was so angry that he tried to charge Burns interest on the sum – £5.10s. Burns naturally refused to pay and is alleged to have said, 'Considering that the money was due by one poet for putting a tombstone over another, he may with grateful surprise thank Heaven that he ever saw a farthing of it.' A rather splendid footnote, recorded on a plaque at the grave, shows that yet another poet tried to get in on the act. Robert Louis Stevenson offered to pay for the refurbishment of the grave, but died before it was completed.

Stevenson, one might say in parentheses, himself wrote one startlingly good epitaph; it appears in 'A Christmas Sermon':

> *Here lies one who meant well, tried a little, failed much:* –
> *Surely that may be his epitaph, of which he need not be ashamed.*

Scotland, of course, had rather inflated ideas for Burns's own epitaph. He died in 1796 but in 1815 was re-buried in a grand mausoleum, which cost every penny of £1500:

> Consigned to earth here rests the lifeless clay,
> Which once a vital spark from heaven inspired!
> The lamp of genius shone full bright as day,
> Then left the world to mourn its light retired.
>
> While beams that splendid orb which lights the sphere,
> While mountain streams descend to swell the main,
> While changeful seasons mark the rolling years –
> Thy fame, O Burns, let Scotia still retain.

On the whole I prefer the more fulsome memorial to a Scotsman, who believed, as I do, in free entry to museums. I am sure Burns would have been most unappreciative of Mr Baillie:

> Here rests
> George Baillie
> a member of the Faculty of
> Procurators of Glasgow
> and
> one of the sheriffs substitute of
> the county of Perth,
> who some years before his death
> divested himself of all his large fortune to endow
> Baillie's Institution
> for promoting the intellectual culture of the operative classes
> in Glasgow, by means of
> Free public Libraries, Reading Rooms and Unsectarian schools
> in the city and suburbs
> under the management of the Faculty, by whom,
> with Special Permission of the Crown,
> This monument is erected here.
>
> May it be an incentive to others to imitate
> this rare example of self-sacrifice and benevolence
> He died 8th Feby 1873 in his 89th year.
>
> Glasgow Cathedral

Burns might, however, have approved of a simple Scottish epitaph, said to be in Kells Churchyard:

Jean Sloan
Died Oct. 6, 1732
Death's steps
are swift,
and yet no nois
maks.
His hands unseen,
and yet
Most shurely
taks.

Only in Scotland do we find true frankness in stone, as on this example quoted by Pettigrew from Northmaven, Shetland:

M.S.
Donald Robertson,
Born 1st of January 1785; died 4th of June 1848
aged 63 years
He was a peaceable quiet man, & to all appearance a sincere Christian.
His death was very much regretted, which was caused by the stupidity of
Laurence Tulloch, of Clotherton, who sold him nitre instead of Epsom
salts, by which he was killed in the space of 3 hours after taking a dose
of it.

The Irish naturally are perhaps more perverse than the Scots:

Here lie the remains of Thomas Nichols
Who died in Philadelphia, March 1753.
Had he lived he would have been buried here.

Kilkeel, Co. Down

Philadelphia, incidentally, seems to many a dream – or perhaps nightmare – town. One great American published his own epitaph in *Vanity Fair* in June 1925:

Here lies W. C. Fields. I would rather be living in Philadelphia.

Dean Swift of St Patrick's Cathedral, Dublin, was second only to Burns as the master of the blistering epitaph; here he is on the Bishop of Salisbury, Gilbert Burnet (1643–1715), who had a very mixed reputation. (One contemporary wrote of him that 'he was zealous for the truth but in telling it always turned it into a lye; he was bent to do good, but fated to mistake evil for it'.)

Here Sarum lyes
who was as wise
And learned as Tom Aquinas
Lawn sleeves he wore
Yet was no more
A Christian than Socinus

Oaths pro and con
He Swallow'd down
Loved Gold like any layman
Wrote, preached and pray'd
And yet betrayed
God's Holy Church for Mammon

Of every Vice
He had a Spice
Altho' a learned Prelate
And yet he dyed
If not belyed
A true Dissenting Zealote

If such a Soule
To heaven he's stole
And scaped old Satan's clutches
We then assume
There may be room
For M[arlborough] and his D[uches]s

Burnet did not get a fair epitaph until 1960, when an American descendant erected a slab in Salisbury Cathedral which put the record of this great historian in a better light:

Gilbert
Burnet
Bishop of Salisbury
1689–1715: Chancellor
of the Most Noble
Order of the Garter
Historian of his times.
Advocate of toleration
Chairman of the Commission
of the Bill of Rights
Organiser of
Queen Anne's Bounty

36

One of the epitaphs ascribed to Swift is nearly as good as Burns at his best:

> Here lies the body of John Shine,
> Who was no Jew for he ate swine;
> He was no Papist for he had no merit;
> He was no Quaker for he had no spirit;
> For forty years he lived and lied,
> For which God damned him as he died.

Swift's own epitaph, on a wall plaque in his cathedral in Dublin, is in Latin, so I shall forbear to quote it.

The English can also join this game. Even in the middle of the puritan Commonwealth bawdy creeps in:

> Here lyeth the body of Eliz. Alleyn.
> She dyed 9 May 1652
> Death here advantage hath of life I spye
> One husband with 2 wifes at once may lye.

Great Witchingham, Norfolk

Soft-ground etching after Thomas Gainsborough.
A shepherd ponders an inscription on a tombstone.

John Dale, barber-surgeon, was buried in Bakewell, Derbyshire, some eighty years later and his memorial expresses a similar theme with rather more sensitivity:

> Know posterity, that on the 8th of April in the year of Grace 1737, the rambling remains of the above said John Dale were, in the 86th yeare of his pilgrimage, laid upon his two wives.

> This thing in life might raise some jealousy,
> Here all three lie together lovingly,
> But from embraces here no pleasure flows,
> Alike are here all human joys and woes;
> Here Sarah's chiding John no longer hears,
> And old John's rambling Sarah no more fears;
> A period's come to all their toilsome lives,
> The good man's quiet; still are both his wives.

An English ideal is expressed in this epitaph which was apparently at Great Wolford, Warwickshire:

> Here Old John Randall lies,
> Who counting from his tale,
> Lived three score years and ten,
> Such virtue was in Ale.
> Ale was his meat,
> Ale was his drink,
> Ale did his heart revive;
> And if he could have drunk his Ale,
> He still had been alive;
> But he died January five
>   1699.

Not so, however, a (surely invented) memorial which Orchard ascribes to Rathly (wherever that may be):

> Here lies Peg, that drunken sot,
> Who dearly loved her jug and pot;
> There she lies as sure can be,
> She killed herself by drinking brandy.

Different people have different tastes:

> . . . Also her son, Peter Brown,
> who fell a victim to the allurements

of the Ice, whilst Skating on the
Serpentine River, December 5th 1796.
Aged 19 years.

Not only were the English often pompous

Virgil Pimfrit, Gent,
Liv'd so Respected
That when the Sable-train of his Mourning Friends
Attended his breathless Corpse
Here to be Entomb'd
Each tearful Eye seemed to Say
There Goes an Honest Man. 1765. Aged 77.

Lamberhurst, Kent

but they occasionally – even well into the twentieth century – produced some stunningly bad verse:

In ever loving memory
of
Samuel Charles May.
The beloved husband of
Harriet Hannah May
Who died May 18th 1923
Aged 63 years.
His Anchor was the Holy Word
His Rudder Blooming Hope
The love of God his maintops'll
And Faith his Sailing Rope.

Southwold, Suffolk

Even the Manx can produce verse that qualifies for The Stuffed Owl; although in various forms it is found throughout the kingdom:

Here lie the Remains
of Paul Gelling of Douglas,
Isle of Man,
who was unfortunately drowned
on his passage from Whitehaven
to the afore-said place the 21st
of October 1834 in the 56th
Year of his age

Tho' boreas blasts and neptunes waves
Have toss'd him to and fro
In spite of both by God's decree
He is harbour'd here below
Here at anchor he does sleep
With many of the fleet
Yet once again he will set sail
His Saviour Christ to meet

Kirk Braddan, Isle of Man

Allegedly at Kingsbridge, Devon, is this careful inscription (also attributed to other places):

Underneath Lieth the Body of Robert Commonly Called Bone Philip who died July 27th 1793 Aged 63 Years At whose request the following lines are here inserted:
Here lie I at the Chancel door
Here lie I because I'm poor
The further in the more you'll pay
Here lie I as warm as they.

The English love large characters, as witness the remarkable Daniel Lambert:

In memory of that prodigy in nature
Daniel Lambert
a native of Leicester,
who was possessed of an excellent and convivial mind, and
in personal greatness had no competitor.
He measured three feet one inch round the leg, nine feet four
inches round the body, and weighed 52 stones 11lbs.
(14lb to the stone)
He departed this life on the 21st of June, 1809, aged 39 years.
As a testimony of respect, this stone was erected by his
friends in Leicester.

St Martin's, Stamford, Lincolnshire

They also like to complain. This is taken from J. D. Briscoe's *History of Bolton* and apparently was preserved in Bolton churchyard:

John Okey
The servant of God was born in London, 1608, came into this toune in
1629, married Mary, daughter of James Crompton, of Breightmet, 1635,
with whome he lived comfortably 20 yeares, & begot 4 sons and 6

40

daughters. Since then he lived sole till the day of his death. In his time were many great changes, & terrible alterations – 18 yeares Civil *Wars* in England, besides many dreadful sea fights – the crown or command of England changed 8 times, Episcopacy laid aside 14 yeares; London burnt by Papists & more stately built again; Germany wasted 300 miles; 200,000 protestants murdered in Ireland, by the papists; this toune thrice stormed – once taken, & plundered. He went throw many troubles and divers conditions, found rest, joy & happines only in holines – the faith fear and love of God in Jesus Christ. He died the 29 of *Ap* and lieth here buried, 1684. Come Lord Jesus, O come quickly. Holiness is man's happiness.

The English are great rabble rousers – even though they do not throw paving stones about with the abandon of their continental neighbours. The story of Queen Caroline is perhaps the most unsavoury of all royal scandals. Nobody came well out of it – the king, the queen, the politicians, the lawyers and even the British public, who demonstrated at her funeral:

Here lies interred the mortal remains of
Richard Henry, Carpenter,
aged 36 years, and of
George Francis, Bricklayer, aged 43 years,
who were slain on the 14th of August 1821, while attending
the funeral of Caroline, of Brunswick,
Queen of England.

The details of that melancholy event belong to the history of the country in which they will be recorded, together with public opinion decidedly expressed relative to the disgraceful transactions of that disastrous day. Deeply impressed with their fate, unmerited and unavenged, their respective trades interred them at their general expense on the 24th day of the same month. Richard Honey left one female orphan. George Francis a widow and three children.

Victims like these, have fallen in every age
To stretch of power or party's cruel rage,
Until even-handed justice comes at last
T'amend the future and avenge the past.
Their friends and fellow men lament their doom,
Protect their orphans, and erect their tomb.

Hammersmith Parish Church

41

They worry about the demon drink; this one probably comes from Lancashire and may never have been carved:

> Here lies the Body of
> John Wiggelsworth,
> More than fifty years he was the
> perpetual Innkeeper in this Town.
> Withstanding the temptations of that dangerous calling,
> he maintained good order in his
> House, kept the Sabbath day Holy,
> frequented the Public Worship
> with his family, induced his guests
> to the same and regularly
> partook of the Holy Communion.
> He was bountiful to the Poor,
> in private as well as in public,
> and, by the blessings of Providence
> on a life so spent, died
> possessed of competent Wealth,
> Feb. 28, 1813,
> aged 77 years.

But they also adore a character who occasionally takes a drop too much (especially one with a bit of class). According to Orchard the following epitaph comes from Hendon:

> In memory of
> Robert Thomas Crossfield M.D.
> son of the late Francis Crossfield,
> of Spinnithorn, in the county of York,
> who died 8th Nov 1802,
> Aged 44 years.
> Beneath this stone Tom Crossfield lies,
> Who cares not now who laughs or cries.
> He laugh'd when sober, and when mellow
> Was a har'em-scar'em heedless fellow,
> He gave to none design'd offence,
> So honi soit qui mal y pense.

The Americans naturally never do things by halves; this one allegedly comes from Coventry, Connecticut:

This monument is erected in
Memory of Capt. Joseph Talcott,
Who was Casually Drowned in the
Proud Waters of the Scungamug River
On the 10th Day of June 1789.
In the 62nd year of his age.

Some epitaphs are rather more cursory; Ravenshaw (who is usually reliable) quotes this:

Received of Philip Harding
his borrowed earth.
July 4th 1673

Crudwell, Wiltshire

A really short auto-epitaph is that of the worthy Dr Fuller, author of Fuller's Worthies:

Fuller's earth.

And I wonder whether there really was a grave with the inscription:

Thorpe's corpse.

IV
THE GREAT AND THE GOOD

The most distinguished epitaph in the British Isles is undoubtedly that of Sir Christopher Wren in St Paul's Cathedral. It is unfortunately written in Latin, but the last line must be quoted because of its absolute distinction:

Si monumentum requiris circumspice

which might be translated, 'If you want a monument, look around'.

Ben Jonson, on the other hand, achieved his famous short epitaph by accident. The outbreak of the Civil War prevented the construction of a larger monument for which money had been collected. The small stone which was placed over his coffin (he was buried in an upright position) was provided with what was intended to be a temporary epitaph:

O rare Ben Jonson!

at the behest of Sir Jack Young, who passed the grave in Westminster Abbey whilst it was being filled in, and paid eighteen pence to have the inscription cut. In the middle of the eighteenth century a more 'fitting' monument was constructed in Poets' Corner, but the original inscription was fortunately retained and can be seen built into the wall of the bench on the north side of the aisle, not far from his grave.

Modern poets have never achieved (or perhaps have not been allowed to achieve) such wit when commemorated in Poets' Corner in Westminster Abbey. The following is reasonably typical of the red tape of this part of the south-east transept:

44

Henry James
O.M.
Novelist
New York 1843
London 1916

In earlier times, however, more licence was allowed a poet's executors, and although many famous English poets are commemorated in the Latin language (Chaucer, Cowley, Dryden, for example), some have been doggerelised in the vernacular by their memorialists:

Michael Draiton Esqr. *A memorable poet of this age,*
Exchanged his laurel for a Crowne of Glorie, Ano, 1631.
Doe pious marble: let thy readers knowe,
What they, and what their children owe
To Draiton's name, whose sacred dust
Wee recommend unto thy trust;
Protect his memr'y and preserve his storye,
Remaine a lastinge monument of his glorye;
And when thy ruines shall disclaime
To be the treas'rer of his name;
His name, that cannot fade, shall be
An everlasting MONUMENT to thee.

Westminster Abbey

Alexander Pope did rather well for James Craggs in Westminster Abbey, signing the verse on his friend's monument:

Statesman, yet Friend to Truth, of Soul sincere
In Action faithful and in Honour clear
Who broke no Promise, serv'd no private end
Who gain'd no Title, and who lost no Friend
Ennobled by Himselfe, by all approv'd
Prais'd, wept and honour'd by the Muse he lov'd.

On the whole that splendid novelist Aphra Behn was probably better served on her much worn tombstone in the cloisters of the Abbey:

Mrs Aphra Behn
Dyed April 16
1689.
Here lies a Proof that Wit can never be
Defence enough against Mortality.

Perhaps it is better not to set a rhymster to work on a poet's memorial. This epitaph – originally commissioned by the Lady Anne Clifford – was so prized that it was restored with its original inscription by private subscription in 1778:

Here lyes (expecting the second Comminge of our Saviour Christ Iesus)
the body of Edmond Spencer, the Prince of Poets in his tyme; whose
divine spirrit needs noe othir witnesse then the works he left behinde him.
He was borne in London in the yeare 1510 and died in the yeare 1596.

Westminster Abbey

Some modern memorials to poets do, however, touch a chord; this is surely one of the great epitaphs of Poets' Corner:

My Subject is War, and the pity of War.
The poetry is in the pity.
Richard Aldington, Laurence Binyon, Edmund Blunden, Rupert Brooke,
Wilfred Gibson, Robert Graves, Julian Grenfell, Ivor Gurney, David Jones,
Robert Nichols, Wilfred Owen, Herbert Read, Isaac Rosenberg, Siegfried
Sassoon, Charles Sorley, Edward Thomas.   1914–1918

There is no indication of who caused this splendidly designed stone to be carved; not so the inscription under the bust simply inscribed:

MILTON

In the year of our Lord Jesus Christ
One thousand seven hundred and thirty and seven
This Bust
of the Author of Paradise Lost
was placed here by William Benson Esquire
One of the two Auditors of the Imprests
to his Majesty King George the second
formerly
Surveyor General of the Works
to his Majesty King George the first.
Rysbrack
was the Statuary who cut it.

Mr Benson certainly got into the act, and, because in so doing he destroyed some verses of Dryden, he also got into *The Dunciad*:

On Poets' tombs see Benson's Titles writ!

Coloured aquatint of Poets' Corner in Westminster Abbey by J. Bluck after A. Pugin in 1811. On the left John Dryden is commemorated. On the far wall plaques celebrate Ben Jonson (left, above the door), Samuel Butler (top, centre), John Milton (top right) and below him Thomas Gray. From volume II of the *History of the Abbey Church of St Peter's, Westminster* of 1812.

Pope himself, great writer of epitaphs, eschewed Westminster. Although he wrote this quatrain which appears as a memorial to him in Twickenham Parish Church, he stated in his will that only the date of his death and his age at death should be inscribed on his tomb:

> *Heroes and Kings! your distance keep:*
> *In peace let one poor Poet sleep,*
> *Who never flatter'd Folks like you:*
> *Let Horace blush, and Virgil too.*

Shakespeare, too, lies outside London. Although a memorial was put up to him in Westminster Abbey in 1740, his true epitaph is to be seen in Stratford below an alabaster bust by Gerard Johnson, which (says Nikolaus Pevsner) makes 'the bard look a self-satisfied schoolmaster':

> *Stay Passenger, why goest thou by so fast,*
> *Read if thou canst, who envious death has plast,*
> *Within this monument Shakespeare: with whome,*
> *Quick nature dide: whose name doth deck this tombe,*
> *Far more, then cost: Sieh all, that he hath Writt*
> *Leaves living art, but page, to serve his Witt.*

Thomas Gray naturally was buried anonymously, but in an adjoining field at Stoke Poges is a substantial memorial, bearing this inscription:

> This Monument, in honour of
> Thomas Gray
> *Was erected A.D.1799*
> Among the scenery
> *Celebrated by that great Lyric and Elegiac Poet.*
> He died in 1771
> And lies unnoticed in the adjoining Churchyard;
> Under the tombstone
> On which he piously and pathetically
> Recorded the interment
> Of his Aunt and lamented Mother

The atheist gets short shrift in the average graveyard. James Baskerville, the typographer (1706–75), was buried in a stone tomb on the site of an old mill in his garden. It has long since disappeared, his body allegedly being reburied on a piece of land near Cradley Chapel. Instead of a cross the tomb was capped by a cone and bore this inscription:

Stranger
Beneath this cone in unconsecrated ground
a friend to the liberties of mankind directed his body to be inurn'd
May the example contribute to emancipate thy mind
From the idle fears of Superstition
And the wicked arts of Priesthood

In private duty bound this book should record the memorial inscription of the founder of the British Museum in the cemetery of Chelsea Old Church:

To the memory of
Sir Hans Sloane, Bart.
President of the Royal Society, and the
College of Physicians,
Who in the year of our Lord 1753
Without the least pain of body, and with a
conscious serenity of mind,
ended a virtuous and beneficent life,
This monument was erected by his two daughters,
Elizabeth Cadogan and Sarah Stanley.

That strange man – poet and politician – Andrew Marvell died within a few yards of the house that was to become the British Museum, on the north side of Great Russell Street on 16 August 1678. He was buried in St Giles-in-the-Fields apparently without a monument. Hull Corporation voted him a monument (he was MP for the city), but this, like so many others, was never erected. His nephew William Popple composed an epitaph which in a rather abbreviated form was placed in 1764 in the newly-built church:

Near unto this place lyeth the body of *Andrew Marvell esquire, a man so endowed by nature, so improved by education, study & travell, so consummated by practice & experience; that joining the most peculiar graces of wit & learning with a singular penetration, & strength of judgment, & excercising all these in the whole course of his life, with an unalterable steadiness in the ways of virtue, he became the ornament and example of his age; beloved by good men, feared by bad, admir'd by all, tho imitated alass by few, & scarce fully paralleled by any, but a tombstone can neither contain his character, nor is marble necessary to transmit it to posterity, it will always be legible in his inimitable writings, he served the town of Kingston upon Hull, above 20 years successively in Parliament, & that, with such wisdom, dexterity, integrity and courage as becomes a true patriot, He dyed the 16. August 1678 in the 58th year of his age.*

It was not only poets whose bodies or memorials did not end up in the Abbey; Sir Winston Churchill, for example, was buried at Bladon. Not so some others:

Erected by
the King and Parliament
as a testimony to
The Virtues and Abilities
of
William Pitt, Earl of Chatham
During whose Administration
In the Reigns of George the Second and George the Third
Divine Providence
exalted Great Britain
to an Height of Prosperity and Glory
unknown to any former age

Westminster Abbey

The Earl of Egmont had a different view of this hero:

His rhetoric and power of speech was in abuse only, . . . an arrogance of nature bore him up under the marks of displeasure and contempt for his opinions and his conduct which he often encountered.

Many other politicians are memorialised in Westminster Abbey – they all aim for it! Appropriately the left hand side of the nave as one enters by the west door is full of memorials to the great Socialist dead – the Webbs, Attlee, Ramsay MacDonald and:

The Right Hon.
Ernest Bevin
M.P. Trade Unionist
and statesman
1881–1951

They are nicely placed somewhat to the left of David Lloyd George. Fox was of course buried in the Abbey, but there is a fine plaque to him in Chertsey:

To the
Memory of the Best of Husbands and
The most excellent of Men,
Charles James Fox,
who died sep 13th, 1806

50

And is buried in Westminster Abbey.
His most affectionate wife
Places this Tablet.

Not all politicians make it to Westminster and pompousness is not reserved for the English pantheon:

Charles Watson Wentworth
Marquis of Rockingham, Earl of Malton,
Viscount Higham of Higham Ferrers,
Baron of Buckingham, Malton, Wath, and
Harowden and Baronet in Great Britain,
Earl and Baron of Malton in the
Kingdom of Ireland, Lord Lieutenant and
Custos Rotulorum of the West Riding
of Yorkshire, City of York and County
of the same, Custos Rotulorum of the
North Riding, and Vice Admiral of the
Maritime parts therof, High Steward
of Kingston upon Hull, Knight of the
Garter and first Commissioner of the
Board of Treasury.
Born May 24th 1730, died July 12 1782.

The Rockingham Mausoleum, Wentworth Woodhouse

The mausoleum cost £3,208, exclusive of the sculpture and the architect's fees – almost as extravagant as some of the most expansive epitaphs. This is perhaps why aristocrats and politicians lend themselves to the sort of cod epitaphs to be seen in the last chapter of this book. Some, however, are rather nicer than others. Edward Courtenay, Earl of Devonshire, was not buried in Westminster Abbey; he died in 1419 and was buried in Tiverton parish church. Ravenshaw records part of his epitaph, which disappeared when the medieval Courtenay chapel was demolished in the eighteenth century:

Hoe, hoe, who lies here
I the goode Erle of Devonshire
With Maud my wyff to mee ful deere
We lyved togeather fyfty fyve yeare.
   What we gave, we have,
   What we spent, we hade,
   What we lefte that we loste.

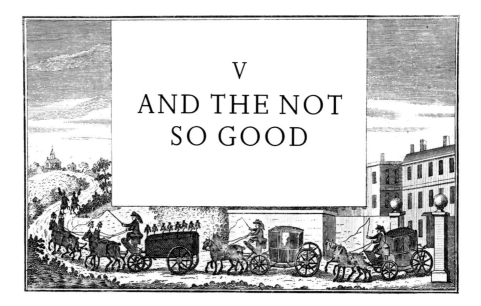

V
AND THE NOT SO GOOD

The truly wicked rarely get their just deserts on their funerary memorials. Their epitaphs tend to be published in the prints. One such concerns a most notorious character of the eighteenth century, who was found guilty of everything from rape to peculation, and who had the financial morals of a bucket-shop alley-cat. In 1732, when he died, John Arbuthnot wrote (with only a little exaggeration) in *The Gentleman's Magazine* on the not much lamented Colonel Charteris (later memorialised in no uncertain fashion by Pope):

> Here continueth to rot
> The body of Francis Chartres;
> *Who with an inflexible constancy and in-*
> *imitable uniformity of life, persisted,*
> *in spite of age and infirmities,*
> In the practice of every human vice,
> Excepting prodigality and hypocrisy:
> His insatiable avarice exempted him from the first
> His matchless impudence from the second.
> *Nor was he more singular in the undeviating pravity*
> *of his manners, than successful in accumulating wealth:*
>
> For without trade or profession,
> *Without trust of publick money,*
> *And without bribe-worthy service,*
> He acquired, or more properly created,
> *A ministerial estate.*

He was the only person of his time
Who could cheat without the mask of honesty,
Retain his primeval meanness when Possessed of
ten thousand a year;
And having daily deserved the gibbet for what he
did,
Was at last condemned to it for what he could not do.

O indignant reader!
Think not his life useless to mankind!
Providence connived at his execrable designs,
To give after-ages a conspicuous proof and
example
Of how small estimation is exorbitant wealth
in the sight of God, by bestowing it on the
most unworthy of mortals.

Murderer and victim are not often commemorated on the same stone, nor interred in the same grave, but:

Here two young Danish Souldiers lye
The one in quarrell chanced to die;
The others Head by their own Law,
With Sword was sever'd at one Blow.
December the 23d
1689

St Mary's, Beverley, Yorkshire

The following epitaph is said to come from Bury St Edmunds; it sounds convincing enough:

Sarah Lloyd
On the 23rd April 1800
In the 22nd year of her age
Suffered a just and ig-
nominious death
for admitting her
Abandoned seducer
In the dwelling house of her
Mistress on the
3rd of October 1799
& becoming the instrument

In his hands of the crime of
Robbery & Housebreaking.

These were her last words:
May my example be a warning to thousands.

Pettigrew – who is never very hot on his provenances – records the following inscription from a place that apparently does not exist – Horsley Down, Cumberland. It is a pity, for the inscription – if long – is worthy of record:

Here lie the bodies
Of Thomas Bond and Mary his wife.
She was temperate, chaste and charitable;

BUT

She was proud, peevish, and passionate.
She was an affectionate wife, and a tender mother:

BUT

Her husband and child, whom she loved,
Seldom saw her countenance without a disgusting frown,
Whilst she received visitors, whom she despised with an
endearing smile.
Her behaviour was discreet towards strangers;

BUT

Independent in her family.
Abroad, her conduct was influenced by good breeding;

BUT

At home, by ill temper.
She was a professed enemy to flattery,
And was seldom known to praise or commend;

BUT

The talents in which she principally excelled,
Were differences of opinion, and discovering flaws and
imperfections.
She was an admirable economist,
And, without prodigality,
Dispensed plenty to every person in her family;

BUT

Would sacrifice their eyes to a farthing candle.
She sometimes made her husband happy with her good qualities;

BUT

Much more frequently miserable – with her many failings;

Insomuch that in thirty years cohabitation he often
lamented
That maugre of all her virtues,
He had not, in the whole, enjoyed two years of matrimonial
comfort.

AT LENGTH
Finding that she had lost the affections of her husband,
As well as the regard of her neighbours,
Family disputes having been divulged by servants,
She died of vexation, July 20th 1768,
Aged 48 years.
Her worn out husband survived her four months and two days,
And departed this life, Nov. 28 1768
In the 54th year of his age.
William Boyd, brother of the deceased, erected this stone,
As a weekly monitor, to the surviving wives of this parish,
That they may avoid the infamy
Of having their memories handed to posterity
With a Patch Work character.

Sir William Alexander, Earl of Stirling and Viscount Canada (no less), was quite a distinguished character – poet, courtier, administrator, colonist. He died in penury in London in 1640 and was buried in Stirling. His achievements hardly – to our eyes – merit this anonymous epitaph:

Heir layes a fermer and a millar,
A poet and a psalme book spillar,
A purchaser by hooke and crooke,
A forger of the service booke,
A coppersmith quho did much evil
A friend to bischopes and the devill;
A vain ambitious flattering thing,
Late secretary for a king.
Some tragedies in verse he pen'd
At last he made a tragicke end.

This epitaph should not properly be placed in this section, but the couplet persuaded me. It was in St Anne's, Aldersgate, London:

Peter Heiwood, younger son of Peter Heiwood, one of the Counsellors of
Jamaica, by Grace, Daughter of Sir John Muddeford, Knight and Baronet,
Great Grandson of Peter Heiwood of Haywood in the County Palatine of

55

Lancaster; who apprehended Guy Faux, with his dark Lanthorn. And for his zealous Prosecution of Papists, as Justice of the Peace, was stabbed in Westminster Hall, by John James a Dominican Friar, Anno Dom. 1640. Obiit Novem. 2 1701.

Reader, if not a Papist bred,
Upon such Ashes gently tread.

Westminster Abbey may play host to the bodies of many rogues, but few can have been as nasty a piece of work as Thomas Thynne, although his epitaph and his memorial imply that he was wrongly done by. Thynne, with his £10,000 a year, secretly married a rich heiress, the Countess of Ogle. The marriage was not consummated and the lady left for the Continent, lured by the wiles of the Count Königsmark. Thynne – no gentleman – did not respond to offers of duels, but dispatched three thugs to France. They attempted to kill the Count but failed, whereupon Königsmark came to England with three toughs of his own and killed Mr Thynne in Pall Mall, 'by discharging a Musquetoon into [his] coach'. Königsmark and his ruffians were taken at Gravesend and, although the three hired hands were executed, the noble seducer escaped the rope. Thynne's death was regarded as 'a just Reward for his Perfidy, in having, at the Duke of Monmouth's request, debauch'd a young Lady of Character, basely deserting her; whence came the Saying, *That he had escaped this danger, if he had either married the Woman he had lain with, or lain with the Lady he had married*'. The memorial (which is figured by Dart, who recounts the story with great gusto) shows a dying Thynne, of unpleasant countenance, reclining above a marble relief of the scene in Pall Mall. An epitaph was designed for the monument but prohibited by the authorities (one wonders what lies it told); a small plaque records:

Tho. Thynn of Long Leate
in Com:Wilts Esq: Who was
Barbarously Murdered on
Sunday the 12 of Februa 1682

After which the sins of Peter White of Applegarth, Dumfries, seem praiseworthy:

Beneath this stone lies Peter White
For all the ills he got the wight,
For stealing sheep, and kye and corn,
The like of him was never known.

56

From Sheldon in Vermont comes a splendid case of the biter bit:

Unknown man shot in
the Jennison & Gallup Co's store
while in the act of burglarizing
the safe Oct. 13, 1905.
(Stone bought with money
found on his person.)

And from the Wild West – from Tombstone, Arizona:

Dan Doud
Rex Sample
Tex Howard
Bill Delaney
Dan Kelley
Legally
hanged
Mar. 8 1884

Another from Tombstone tells a different story (both these are quoted by Shushan):

George Johnson
Hanged by mistake

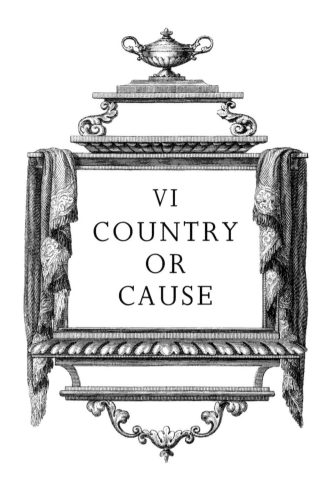

VI
COUNTRY
OR
CAUSE

The death of those who fought in foreign lands is properly remembered in epitaphs, which vary from the banal to the sublime. The most moving is certainly that which appears most commonly on the well-designed grave-stones erected over the unidentified dead of the British Army in two world wars:

> *A soldier of the Great War.*
> *Known unto God.*

The British Museum was coincidentally involved in one of the best-known epitaphs of the First World War. The poet Laurence Binyon was a member of the staff of the Museum and in 1914 wrote a poem entitled 'For the Fallen'. Not perhaps one of his best works in its entirety, it included, however, a stanza which is entirely memorable and was much used on war memorials, including that of the Museum itself:

They shall grow not old, as we that are left grow old:
Age shall not weary them, nor the years condemn.
At the going down of the sun and in the morning
We will remember them.

A. E. Housman did in totality rather better in his 'Epitaph on an Army of Mercenaries':

These, in the day when heaven was falling,
The hour when earth's foundations fled,
Follow'd their mercenary calling
And took their wages and are dead.

Their shoulders held the sky suspended;
They stood, and earth's foundations stay;
What God abandon'd, these defended,
And saved the sum of things for pay.

Housman also wrote the lines inscribed on a plaque in the British War Cemetery on Vis in the Adriatic:

Here dead we lie, because we did not choose
To live and shame the land from which we sprung;
Life, to be sure, is nothing much to lose,
But young men think it is, and we were young.

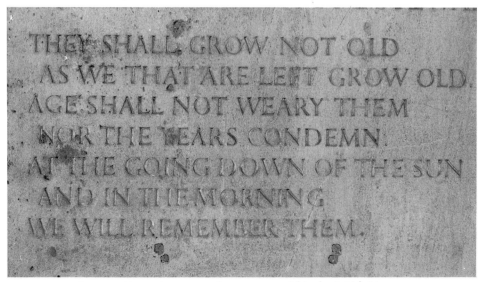

Laurence Binyon's verse on the war memorial in the British Museum.

Even today such memorials can be erected and still have the power to move the reader; this one is recorded by Lamont-Brown:

As the days roll by, this day we do recall.
The noonday sun.
The twittering of strange birds.
The brown meandering stream, that heard the din of battle
And carried you to history, to join the brave.
That swords be turned into ploughshares.

Erected by the people of Camolin and comrades
To the memory of Trooper Edward Gaffney, Norrismount.
Killed in the Congo (Zaire) on the 13th September 1961
In the cause of world peace.

Church of the Immaculate Conception, Camolin, Co. Wexford

Scotland is the home of the British soldier and the memorials are quite frightening in their detail:

To the memory of
Two officers
Twenty one serjeants, twenty seven
corporals, nine drummers, four hundred and
thirty nine privates, forty seven women
and twenty one children of the seventy
eighth Highland Regiment, in all amounting
to six hundred and sixty nine, who died on
the banks of the River Indus in Sinde,
between the sixth day of September one
thousand eight hundred and forty four and
the fourth day of March one thousand eight
hundred and forty five.

St Giles's Cathedral, Edinburgh

The death of soldiers – normally officers – abroad is commemorated in practically every parish church in this country, in more or less fulsome fashion. A modest example occurs in Chelsea Parish Church, but it is only fair to point out that Colonel Cadogan's friends and family were not satisfied with one memorial; he is also commemorated in both St Paul's and Glasgow Cathedral:

To the Memory of
Lieutenant Colonel the Honourable Henry Cadogan,

Of His Majesty's Seventy-first Regiment,
who fell in the battle of Vittoria on 21 June 1813,
in the 33rd year of his age.
The Officers of his Regiment have erected this Monument
In token of their esteem and regard.

One of the grandest memorials in Westminster Abbey, certainly one of the biggest, records the deaths of three sailors. It dominates the west side of the north transept. Carved by that notorious skinflint Joseph Nollekens, it is totally out of harmony with the great church – it would have been better in St Paul's, where indeed such monuments do occur. The inscription smacks of the parliamentary draftsman:

Captain William Bayne,
Captain William Blair,
Captain Lord Robert Manners,
were mortally wounded,
in the course of the naval engagements,
under the command of Sir George Brydges Rodney
on the IXth and XIIth of April MDCCLXXXII.
In memory of their services,
the King and Parliament of Great Britain
have caused this monument to be erected.

Whilst these men died for their country, others died for their cause and the Scots are very good at doing just that. The Covenanters defeated at Bothwell Bridge in 1679 were given no quarter. Some of those captured were brought to Edinburgh, imprisoned near Greyfriars (but not in the area now romantically identified as 'the covenanters' prison') and executed in the Grassmarket. Over a hundred were buried in a trench in Greyfriars Cemetery in an area reserved for common criminals. In 1706 a monument was erected nearby (which was enlarged in 1771). The same epitaph was used on both:

Halt, passenger, take heed what you do see –
This tomb doth show for what some men did die:
Here lies interred the dust of those who stood
Gainst perjury, resisting unto blood:
Adhering to the covenants and laws –
Establishing the same: which was the cause
Their lives were sacrificed unto the lust
Of prelatists abjured – though here their dust
Lies mixt with murderers and other crew
Whom justice justly did to death pursue.

> But as for them no cause was to be found
> Worthy of death: but only they were found
> Constant and steadfast, zealous, witnessing
> For the prerogatives of Christ their King.
> Which truths were sealed by famous Guthrie's head,
> And all – along with Mr Renwick's blood –
> They did endure the wrath of enemies,
> Reproaches, torments, deaths, and injuries.
> But yet they are those who through such trouble came,
> And triumph now in glory with the lamb.

They were preceded to execution by a grandee, whose nineteenth-century monument – itself very grand in its marble and alabaster – is in St Giles's Cathedral nearby:

> Archibald Campbell Marquess of Argyll
> Beheaded near this cathedral A.D.1661
> Leader in council and in field for reformed religion
> 'I see a Crown on the King's Head
> He hastens me to a better
> Crown than his own'

On a park bench (the modern equivalent of a storied urn) in the same town – in Princes Street – is the following inscription to a major cause which certain Scots supported:

> In memory of those who
> left this city to serve
> with the International
> Brigade in the
> Spanish Civil War

One Irishman, whose memorial was once in St Martin-in-the-Fields in London, seemed to know who was to be blamed:

> Sacred
> To the memory of John Irving Esq.
> of Sligo, Ireland
> Surgeon to His Majesty's Forces,
> who died on 22nd of April 1810,
> Aged 33 years;
> A victim like thousands of our
> Gallant Countrymen

To the fatal consequences of the
Unfortunate Expedition to the Scheldt,
Commanded by John, Earl of Chatham.

as did the parents of this American soldier, commemorated in St Albans, Vermont:

Joseph P Brainerd, A Brave Soldier.
Joseph Partridge Brainerd, Son of Joseph Brainerd and his wife Fanny
Partridge, a conscientious, faithful, brave Union Soldier, who was born
on the 27th day of June 1840, graduated from the University of Vermont
in August 1862, enlisted into Co. L of the Vermont Cavalry, was
wounded and taken prisoner by the Rebels in the Wilderness, May 5,
1864, was sent to Andersonville Prison Pen in Georgia where he died on
the 11th day of Sept. 1864 entirely and wholly neglected by President
Lincoln and murdered by the Rebels, with thousands of our loyal Soldiers
by Starvation, Privation and Abuse.

Some soldiers did not die in battle; but sometimes their death was glorious. The quatrain on this stone, said to be in Winchester Cathedral Churchyard, is well known – the full inscription is, however, seldom quoted in its entirety:

In Memory of
THOMAS THETCHER
a grenadier of the Ninth Regiment
of Hants Militia, who died of a
Violent Fever, Contracted by drinking
Small Beer when Hot, the 12th of May
1769. Aged 26 Years.
In Grateful Remembrance of
whose Universal
Goodwill Towards his Comrades
This Stone
Is Placed here at Their Expense
As a Small
Testimony of Their Regard and Concern.
Here sleeps in Peace a Hampshire Grenadier,
Who caught his death by drinking cold small beer.
Soldiers, be wise from his untimely fall,
And when ye're hot drink strong or not at all.

According to Pettigrew this monument was restored by the garrison in 1781, when the following lines were added:

An honest soldier never is forgot
Whether he die by musket or by pot.

That great soldier Sir Walter Raleigh, so it is said, wrote his own epitaph on the night before his execution in 1618; this is one version:

Even such is Time, that takes in trust
Our youth, our joys, our all we have,
And pays us but with age and dust;
Who in the dark and silent grave,
When we have wandered all our ways,
Shuts up the story of our days.
But from the earth, this grave, this dust,
The Lord shall raise me up, I trust.

Airmen do not belong to the heroic period of epitaphs, but not far from the temporary tomb of Oliver Cromwell, behind the high altar of Westminster Abbey, is a chapel of remembrance to the airmen of two World Wars. One of the memorials is a slab in the floor which achieves the real simplicity of fame:

Trenchard
Marshal of the Royal Air Force
1873–1956

Lastly, so that there should be no sexual discrimination:

In Memory of
Phoebe Hessel
Who was born in Stepney in the year 1713
She served for many Years
as a private soldier in the 5th Regt, of foot
in different parts of Europe
and in the year 1745 fought under the command
of the Duke of Cumberland
at the battle of Fontenoy
where she received a Bayonet wound in her Arm.
Her long life which commenced in the time of
Queen Anne
extended to the reign of
George IV

64

by whose munificence she received comfort
and support in her later Years
she died at Brighton, where she had long resided,
December 12th. 1821 *Aged 108 Years*

Brighton Churchyard

An engraved card for Lord Nelson's funeral in 1805.

VII
MECHANICAL
FAILURE

One of the most quoted – and variously provenanced – epitaphs is typical of a group which describe in detail the trade of the person commemorated. This is often done with great – not to say heavy – play on words. Once composed they are found in various guises throughout the country and even in America. This example was copied by Ravenshaw – one of the most painstaking and accurate collectors of epitaphs – in 1857 in Lydford, Devon:

> Here lies in a horizontal position
> The outside case of George Rongleigh, watchmaker,
> Whose abilities in that line were an honor
> to his profession.
> Integrity was the Mainspring
> and Prudence the Regulator
> of all the actions of his life;
> Humane, Generous and Liberal,
> His Hand never stopped
> Till he had relieved distress:
> So nicely were all his Actions regulated
> That he never went wrong,

Except when set going
By People
who did not know his key:
Even then he was easily set right again.
He had the art of disposing his time so well
That his hours glided away
In one continual round
of pleasure and delight,
Till an unlucky minute put a period to
his existence.
He departed this life November 14th, 1802,
Aged 57;
Wound up
In hopes of being taken in hand
by his maker,
And of being thoroughly cleaned and repaired,
and set going
In the World to come.

An early example of this genre can be seen in the cloisters of Westminster Abbey:

With Diligence and Trust most exemplary,
Did *William Lawrence* serve a Prendary;
And for his Pains now past, before not lost,
Gain'd this Remembrance at his Master's Cost.
O! read these Lines again, you seldom find
A servant Faithful, and his Master kind.
Short Hand he wrote, his flower in prime did fade,
And hasty Death short Hand of him hath made.
Well couth he Numbers, and well Measure Land,
Thus doth he now that Ground wheron you stand,
Wherin he lies so Geometrical,
Art maketh some, but thus will Nature all.
Obiit Decemb. 28. 1621. Ætatis suae 29

Typical is this epitaph vaguely located by Pettigrew, 'in a churchyard at Chester':

Here in the grave lies Catherine Gray,
Changed to a senseless lump of clay;
By earth and clay she got her pelf,
And now she's turned to clay herself.

Ye weeping friends, let me advise,
Abate your tears and dry your eyes;
Who knows, but in the course of years,
In some tall pitcher or brown pan,
She in her shop may be again.

The following, said to have been composed by William Hayley (1745–1820) – a poet who might deservedly be described as minor – appears in many versions. This, in memory of Richard Austin, blacksmith, was recorded at Aylesbury:

My Sledge and Hammer lye declin'd,
My Bellows too have lost their wind,
My Fire's extinct, my Forge decaid
And in the dust my Vice is laid.
My Coal is spent, my Iron's gone,
My nail's are drove, my Work is done.

Some craftsmen must have inspired verse simply by the euphony of their names. Mr Spong is memorialised here at Ockham, Surrey, but the verse is found throughout the land:

John Spong, carpenter, died 17 November 1736.
Who many a sturdy oak had laid along,
Fell'd by Death's surer hatchet, here lies Spong.
Posts oft he made, Yet ne'er a place could get,
And liv'd by railing, tho' he was no wit.
Old saws he had, altho' no antiquarian,
And stiles corrected, yet no grammarian.
Long liv'd he Ockham's prime architect;
And lasting as his fame, a tomb t'erect
In vain we seek an artist such as he
Whose pales and gates are for eternity.

At some stage an extra couplet has been added to this epitaph:

So here he rests from all life's toils and follies;
O! spare, kind heav'n, his fellow lab'rer Hollies.

After which doggerel it is pleasant to turn to a master writer. Benjamin Franklin – that great polymath who was always a little too forward for his own good (as witness his autobiography) – wrote his own epitaph which is much quoted and is here spelled out once again. Needless to say it was not used on his tombstone in Christ Church, Philadelphia, about which he gave explicit (and modest) instructions in his will:

The body of
B. Franklin,
Printer,
Like the cover of an old book
its contents torn out,
and stripped of its lettering and gilding,
lies here, food for worms.
But the work shall not be wholly lost,
for it will, as he believed, appear once more,
in a new and more perfect edition,
corrected and amended
by the Author.
He was born Jan 6, 1706.
Died 17

Printers, so used to words, play with them to the end, plagiarising to taste. At least some of them are short, as this one dated to 1818 and said to be in the churchyard at Bury St Edmunds, Suffolk:

Here lie the remains of L. Gedge, Printer.
Like a worn-out character, he has returned to the Founder,
Hoping that he will be re-cast in a better and
more perfect mould.

More of them, as befits their trade, enter into the true spirit of the long and wordy inscription. Andrews recorded this memorial to a printer on *The Coventry Mercury*:

Here
lies inter'd
the mortal remains
of
John Hume,
Printer,
who, like an old worn out type,
battered by frequent use,
reposes in the grave.
But not without the hope that at some future time
he might be cast in the mould of righteousness,
and safely locked up
in the chase of immortality.

He was distributed from the board of life
on the 9th day of Sept., 1827
Aged 75.
Regretted by his employers,
and respected by his fellow artists.

St Michael's, Coventry

Surgeons certainly qualify as mechanics and the following, which could only have been written by a fellow practitioner, is recorded from Harrow Churchyard:

Here lies the Body
Of Mr Thomas Woodward, Surgeon
of Piccadilly
who departed this life Sept 23, 1769

In the 67 Year of his Age

He was Eminent for the Knowledge of
Surgery, having made that Science
His Study for upwards of Forty Years.
In the cure of Ruptures he surpassed all
the Faculty in the Age he Lived.
And all Past Ages, as many thousands
of all Ranks who have been Cured
by his Medicines and Bandages can Ivince.
The poor afflicted with that Disorder
He Cured gratis.

The only dental epitaph known to me is entirely apocryphal, though much repeated:

Stranger! Approach this spot with gravity!
John Brown is filling his last cavity.

Musicians surely qualify under this heading. In 1621 the organist of Norwich Cathedral died and an epitaph was painted on a pillar on the north side of the nave; the last line refers to a painted pair of figures holding laurel wreaths over a corpse:

Here William Inglott organist doth rest
Whose arte in musique this cathedrall blest.
For descant most, for voluntary all
He past: organ, songe and virginall.

70

He left this life at age of thirtie seaven
And now 'mongst angells all sings saints in heaven
His fame flies farr, his name shall never die
See art and age here crowne his memory.

Another organist is commemorated in Wakefield Cathedral:

In memory of
Henry Clemetshaw
upwards of fifty years organist
of this church, who died
May 7, 1821, aged 68 years.
Now, like an organ, robb'd of pipes and breath,
Its keys and stops are useless made by death,
Tho' mute and motionless in ruins laid,
Yet when re-built by more than mortal aid,
This instrument, new voiced, and tuned, shall raise
To God, its builder, hymns of endless praise.

Nobody would call Purcell a mechanic, but his burial in the 'musicians' aisle' of Westminster Abbey triggered some very mechanical epitaphs. His memorial, however, is highly quotable:

Here lyes
Henry Purcell Esqr.
who left this life
And is gone to that blessed place
Where only his Harmony
can be exceeded
Obijt 21 die Novembrs
Anno Ætatis suae 37mo
Annoq Domini 1695

This is much better than that a few yards away recording the life of another great musician in bathetic prose:

SIR
CHARLES
VILLIERS
STANFORD
Born 30th Sept 1852
Died 29th March 1924
A Great
Musician

Next to musicians are parish clerks, a dying race:

Erected
In remembrance of
Philip Roe
who died 12th September 1815
Aged 52 years
The vocal powers here let us mark
Of Philip our late Parish Clerk
In Church none ever heard a Layman
With a clearer Voice say 'Amen!'
Who now with Hallelujahs Sound
Like Him can make the Roofs rebound?
The Choir lament his choral Tones
The Town – so soon Here lie his Bones.
'Sleep undisturb'd within thy peaceful shrine
Till Angels wake thee with such notes as thine.'

Bakewell, Derbyshire

Parsons, bishops and the like have sonorous, pious, religious epitaphs (it is after all their calling). They are also much given to Latin – and even Greek and Hebrew. They nearly always bag the most prominent places in the church, around the apse, and are full of virtue and Oxford and Cambridge degrees. I have been hard pressed to find one of more than pious interest, but the laid-back antiquarian pursuits of the Reverend Mr Leman should commend him to readers of this book:

Sacred to the memory
of the Rev Thomas Leman, of Wenhaston Hall
in this parish,
who died on the 17th day of March 1826;
the last male descendant of his ancient name.
He added to the feelings of a Gentleman,
Talents and Learning without Ostentation,
and Christian Piety without Austerity.
In a curious line of antiquarian research
(The knowledge of Roman Remains in Britain),
he had few superiors;
but in the nobler and more amiable merit
of domestic life
as a husband, a son, a brother, a friend and a master,
he was never exceeded.

We flatter not in the grave:
'He that saw it bears record, and his record is true.'

John xix.25

Wenhaston, Suffolk

The amateur is also sometimes celebrated. This epitaph to Mrs Jane Molony in St George's burial ground in London is variously attributed. In many anthologies it is quoted – rather inaccurately – as the epitaph of 'Lady O'Looney', and said to be at Pewsey. Ravenshaw – whom I would tend to trust – copied it in 1877. Here we can spare space for only a part of this extremely convoluted memorial inscription:

Sacred to the memory of
Mrs Jane Molony
She died in London in January 1839
Aged 74
She was hot, passionate and tender
And a highly accomplished lady and a superb drawer
in water colours which was much admired in the
exhibition rooms in
Somerset House some years past
'Though lost for ever, yet a friend is dear,
The heart yet pays a tributary tear'

Actors' epitaphs lean towards the pompous. But some just avoid it. Unusual is the tombstone in Maggoty Johnson's Wood, Gawsworth, Cheshire, where the last jester in England (by his own account) lies buried by his own request in unconsecrated ground. Samuel Johnson was an actor and playwright whose pseudonym was Lord Flame:

Under this Stone
rest the Remains of Samuel Johnson,
afterwards ennobled with the grander title of
Lord Flame.
Who, after having been in his Life distinct from other men,
By the eccentricities of his Genius,
chose to retain the same Character after his death.
And was on his own Desire buried here May 5th
AD MDCCLXXIII, aged 82.

Stay thou whom chance or ease persuades to seek the quiet of these
*   sylvan shades.*
Here undisturbed hid from vulgar eyes, a wit, musician, poet, player lies.

A dancing master too in grace he shone, and all the arts of opera were his own.

In comedy well skilled, he drew Lord Flame; acted the part and gained himself the name.

Averse to strife how oft he'd gravely say, these peaceful groves should shade his breathless day.

That when he rose again laid here alone, no friend and he should quarrel for a bone.

Thinking that were some old lame gossip nigh, she possibly might take his leg or thigh.

Engineers have been given fulsome epitaphs:

Sacred to the memory of
Matthew Boulton F.R.S
By the skilful exertion of a mind turned to philosophy and mechanics,
the application of a taste correct and refined,
and an ardent spirit of enterprise, he embellished and extended
the arts and manufacture of his country,
leaving his establishment of Soho a noble monument of his
genius, industry and success.
The character his talents had raised, his virtues adorned and exalted.
Active to discover merit, and prompt to relieve distress,
His encouragement was liberal, his benevolence unwearied.
Honoured and admired at home and abroad
He closed a life eminently useful, the 17th of August 1809, aged 81.
Esteemed, loved and lamented.

Handsworth, Birmingham

It is said that Lord Brougham wrote this epitaph to his fellow Scot in West-minster Abbey:

James Watt
Not to perpetuate a name
Which must endure while the peaceful arts flourish,
But to show
That mankind have learned to honour those
Who best deserve their gratitude,
The King
His Ministers and many of the Nobles
and Commons of the Realm,

Raised this monument to
James Watt
Who, directing the force of original genius,
early exercised in Philosophic research
To the improvement of
The Steam Engine
Enlarged the resources of his country,
Increased the power of man
And rose to an eminent place
Among the most illustrious followers of science
And the real Benefactors of the world.
Born at Greenock MDCCXXXVI
Died at Heathfield in Staffordshire, MDCCCXIX.

This epitaph for an engine driver and his mate is allegedly repeated in various guises throughout the kingdom; this one may be seen in Ely Cathedral;

In memory of
William Pickering
Who died Decr. 24th 1845
Aged 50 years.
Also Richard Edger
Who died Decr 24th 1845
Aged 24 years.

The Spiritual Railway
The Line to Heaven by Christ was made
With heavenly truth the Rails are laid.
From earth to heaven the line extends,
To Life Eternal where it ends.
Repentence is the Station then
Where Passengers are taken in.
No fee is there for them to pay,
For Jesus is himself the way.
God's Word is the first Engineer
He points the way to Heaven so dear,
Through tunnels dark and dreary here
It does the way to Glory steer.
God's Love the fire, his Truth the Steam,
Which drives the Engine and the Train.
All you who would to Glory ride,
Must come to Christ, in him abide.

In First, and Second, and Third Class,
Repentence, Faith and Holiness.
You must the way to Glory gain
Or you with Christ will not remain.
Come then poor Sinners, now's the time
At any station on the Line.
If you'll repent and turn from sin
The Train will stop and take you in.

I do not know that I altogether believe this inscription, which is said to be in Bridgetown, Barbados:

Underneath this Tomb
lies interred
The Earthly Remains of
Benjamin Massiah
Late Merchant of this Island
who was universally
Beloved and Respected by
All that knew him and whose
Death
was much lamented.
He had been Reader of the
Jews synagogue
for many years without Fee or Reward
and performed the Office of
Circumciser
with Great Applause
and Dexterity.
He departed this life
On the 29 Adar 5542
Corresponding to
the 15th March
1782
Aged 67 Years and Eight Months

An unusual occupation is recorded by Fritz Spiegl – from Cheltenham:

To the memory of
John Higgs
pig killer
Who died November 26th 1825
Aged 55 Years

Here lies John Higgs
A famous man for killing pigs.
For killing pigs was his delight
Both morning afternoon and night.
Both heat and cold he did endure
Which no Physician could cure.
His knife is laid his work is done
I hope to heaven his soul is gone.

Epitaphs to the memory of sellers of shell-fish are rare:

Mary Atkinson, died Jan. 1. 1786, aged 77
Periwinkles! Periwinkles!
Was ever her cry;
She labour'd to live
Poor and honest to die.
At the last day again
How her old eyes will twinkle;
For no more will she cry
Perwinkle! Periwinkle!

Brighton

There would perhaps be more use for this:

Here lies poor but honest
Bryan Tunstall.
He was a most expert Angler,
until Death, envious of his merit,
threw out his line, hook'd him
and
landed him here the 21st day of April
1790.

Ripon, Yorkshire

I have never to my knowledge been to Upton-upon-Severn in Worcestershire. Perhaps I should, for one of the most frequently quoted epitaphs is alleged to come from there:

Here in the grave, in hope of Zion,
Doth lie the landlord of the Lion.
His son keeps on the business still,
Resigned unto the heavenly will.

Let the Scots have the penultimate word:

Robert Logie
Carpenter
He was a just and pious
man and to say more is un
necessary and to say less
would be ungrateful

Doffus, Morayshire

I have left to the end of this chapter the rather forced epitaph of a great collector of epitaphs, as transcribed by a much later collector, Thomas Pettigrew, who records that it was inscribed at the cost and charge of John Skillicorn in St James's Church, Clerkenwell:

Weever, who laboured in a learned strain,
To make men, long since dead, to live again;
And with expense of oil and ink did watch
From the worm's mouth the sleeping corse to snatch,
Hath by his industry begot a way,
Death (who insidiates all things) to betray;
Redeeming freely by his care and cost
Many a sad herse, which time long since gave lost,
And to forgotten dust such spirit did give,
To make in our memories to live;
For wheresoe'er a ruined tomb he found,

His pen hath built it new out of the ground;
Twixt earth and him this interchange we find,
She hath to him, he been to her like kind;
She was his mother, he, a grateful child,
Made her his theme, in a large work compil'd,
Of funerals, reliques, and brave structures rear'd,
On such as seem'd unto her most endear'd;
Alternately to him a grave she lent,
o'er which his book remains a monument.
   Lancashire gave me breath,
   And Cambridge education;
   Middlesex gave me death,
   And this Church my humation: –
   And Christ to me has given a place in Heaven.
     Ætatis Suae 56, A.D.1632

The Puzzle. A satirical engraving published by J. Bowles in 1756.

THEY SHOULD HAVE DIED HEREAFTER

One of the greatest pleasures of the epitaph hunter is to dig out the might-have-beens: epitaphs to people not yet dead or even to people not yet alive. Archbishop Whately composed one such and entitled it an 'Anticipatory Dirge' – a splendid phrase! Its subject was Dean Buckland, the geologist and also, as his epitaph in Westminster Abbey proudly boasts, a Trustee of the British Museum:

> Mourn, Ammonites, mourn o'er his funeral urn,
>   Whose neck we must grace no more;
> Gneiss, granite and slate – he settled your date,
>   And his ye must now deplore.
>
> Weep, caverns, weep, with infiltering drip,
> Your recesses he'll cease to explore;
> For mineral veins or organic remains,
>   No stratum again will he bore.
>
> His wit shone like crystal – his knowledge profound
>   From gravel to granite descended;
> No trap could deceive him, no slip confound,
>   No specimen true or pretended.

Where shall we our great professor inter,
    That in peace may rest his bones?
If we hew him a rocky sepulchre,
    He'll get up and break the stones,
And examine each stratum that lies around,
For he's quite in his element underground.

If with mattock and spade his body we lay
    In the common alluvial soil;
He'll start up and snatch those tools away
    Of his own geological toil;
In a stratum so young the professor disdains
That embedded should be his organic remains.

Then exposed to the drip of some case-hardening spring,
    His carcase let stalactite cover;
And to Oxford the petrified sage let us bring,
    When duly encrusted all over;
There, 'mid mammoths and crocodiles, high on the shelf,
Let him stand as a monument raised to himself.

In the present spirit of architectural criticism in this country we might recall Abel Evans's verse on Sir John Vanbrugh, architect of Blenheim Palace (in reality it is a parody on an epigram by Martial, on a young slave girl – Erotion – 'let the earth press lightly on her; for she pressed lightly on thee'):

Under this stone, reader, survey
Dead Sir John Vanbrugh's house of clay.
Lie heavy on him, earth! for he
Laid many heavy loads on thee.

A similar sentiment is expressed in kinder fashion on a memorial to Clorinda Haywood, according to Enright, in St Bartholomew's, Edgbaston:

Warm summer sun shine kindly here:
Warm summer wind blow softly here:
Green sod above lie light, lie light:
Good Night, Dear Heart, good night, good night.

Some wrote their own epitaph, as Alexis Piron (1689–1773):

Here lies Piron, a complete nullibiety,
Not even a fellow of a Learned Society.

Dr Johnson, who pontificated – as we have seen – among other things about epitaphs, was himself epitaphed by Soame Jenyns:

> Here lies poor Johnson. Reader! have a care
> Tread lightly, lest you raise a sleeping bear.
> Religious, moral, generous and humane,
> He was, but self-conceited, rude and vain:
> Ill-bred, and overbearing in dispute,
> A scholar and a Christian, yet a brute.
> Would you know all his wisdom and his folly,
> His actions, sayings, mirth and melancholy,
> Boswell and Thrale, retailers of his wit,
> Will tell you how he wrote, and talked, and spit.

The Tudors and Stuarts were rather good at this sort of thing – here an anonymous versifier on Robert Dudley, Earl of Leicester and favourite of Queen Elizabeth I:

> Here lieth the worthy warrior
>   Who never bloodied sword;
> Here lieth the noble counsellor,
>   Who never held his word.
>
> Here lieth his Excellency,
>   Who ruled all the state;
> Here lieth the Earl of Leicester,
>   Whom all the world did hate.

John Wilmot, Earl of Rochester – another royal favourite – wrote an impromptu verse on Charles II, which appears in a number of forms but was originally written as an epitaph:

> Here lies our mutton-eating king,
> Whose word no man relies on;
> Who never said a foolish thing,
> Nor ever did a wise one.

Hanoverian royalty got short shrift from the poets, and shorter from the versifier – this is on Frederick, Prince of Wales, who had the distinction of dying from the bursting of an abcess which had formed as the result of a blow on the head by a tennis ball. It has no known author:

> Here lies Fred
> Who was alive and is dead:

> Had it been his father,
> I had much rather;
> Had it been his brother,
> Still better than another;
> Had it been his sister,
> No one would have missed her;
> Had it been the whole generation,
> So much the better for the nation.
> But since 'tis only Fred,
> Who was alive and is dead,
> There's no more to be said.

Politicians are fair game for the cod epitaph. An anonymous contemporary broadsheet dealt with one senior statesman thus (the epitaph is somewhat shortened):

> Here lies
> LORD CASTLEREAGH
> Who, with scarcely the common qualifications for Power,
> Reached its most commanding altitude:
> and who,
> Protected by the Authority he usurped,
> The intrigues he carried on,
> And the universal Corruption with which he was self-surrounded
> Committed Political Offences,
> Which in most periods of British History,
> Would have subjected him to
> IMPEACHMENT.
> An Irishman by birth: –
> To advance his own private interests and personal ambition,
> He trafficked away
> The last privileges of his Native Land: –
> A MEMBER OF PARLIAMENT
> He disgraced the House and violated the Constitution,
> by bringing to Public Sale
> SEATS IN THE SENATE.
> A MINISTER OF STATE –
> He professed economy, while he practised extravagance;
> Eulogized the Constitution, while he nullified it;
> Most tenacious of his own character,
> He libelled his opponents without decency or reserve.
> Wherever he went,

The loud and hollow blessings of Placemen, Jobbers and Contractors,
(supported and fed by his corruptions,)
Partially drowned
The sincere execrations of that Community
Which has been insulted by his arrogance, impoverished by his Profusion,
And enslaved by his Machinations.
Yielding his Breath,
With much more complacency than he surrendered his Place,
HE DIED
In the very acme of his Political Might,
And
Patronizing Corruption through Life,
He is now become
its victim,
Leaving behind Him,
In the Universal Contempt of Mankind,
For his Political Delinquencies,
AN AWFUL LESSON,
To check the Ambition – qualify the Arrogance – and correct the Infatuation
of
FUTURE MINISTERS!

A shorter, and rather kinder, epitaph by the same hand refers to one of his rivals:

Here lies GEORGE CANNING, a busy pretender,
Of Vice, if in scarlet, a sturdy defender;
A Swiss partizan to Corruption's array,
Who bartered his conscience and battled for pay.
With Castlereagh once, when his courage was up,
By the force of abuse, or the fumes of a cup,
He ventur'd a duel, and found the false lead,
By sympathy swayed, had respect for his head.
In Pensions and Places at length growing old,
He wish'd that his death could by truth be consol'd:
So contempt stepping up, promis'd, ere he was rotten,
His deeds should be quietly curs'd and forgotten.

Even *Private Eye* does not emulate these but the Americans are still at it – this inscription from the 1950s is alleged to be found on a vault in Elgin, Minnesota:

> The Family of Robert T Hallenbeck.
> None of us ever voted for
> Roosevelt or Truman.

And this anonymous couplet on David Lloyd George is worth treasuring:

> Count not his broken pledges as a crime:
> He meant them, HOW he meant them – at the time.

This epitaph for Byng is surely justified, although Voltaire's epigram in *Candide* concerning him is more easily witty – '*Dans ce pays-ci il est bon de tuer de temps en temps un amiral pour encourager les autres*':

> To the perpetual disgrace of public justice,
> The Honourable John Byng, *Vice Admiral of the Blue*,
> fell a martyr to political persecution, March 14,
> in the year 1757;
> when bravery and loyalty were insufficient securities for
> the life and honor of a naval officer.

Another unnecessary death was that of the Earl of Strafford in 1641 – he was in effect condemned by Parliament. Of him Archbishop Laud – himself later beheaded – wrote, 'He served a mild and generous Prince, who knew not how to be, or to be made, great'. Here is John Cleveland's epitaph:

> Here lies wise and valiant dust
> Huddled up 'twixt fit and just,
> Strafford, who was hurried hence,
> 'Twixt treason and convenience.
> He spent his time here in a mist,
> A Papist, yet a Calvinist;
> His Prince's nearest joy and grief,
> He had, yet wanted, all relief;
> The prop and ruin of the State,
> The people's violent love and hate;
> One in extremes loved and abhorred.
> Riddles lie here, or in a word,
> Here lies blood, and let it lie
> Speechless still, and never cry.

The Marquis of Montrose wrote the following (it is said with the point of his sword) after the execution of Charles I, the man who had let Strafford go to his death. Montrose himself was later hanged 'in his red scarlet cassock' in the Grassmarket in Edinburgh:

> Great! Good! and Just! could I but rate
> My Griefs and thy too rigid Fate,
> I'd weep the world to such a strain,
> As it should deluge once again: –
> But since thy loud-tongu'd Blood demands Supplies
> More from Briareus' Hands than Argus' Eyes,
>
> I'll sing thy Obsequies with Trumpets' Sounds,
> And write thy Epitaph with Blood and Wounds.

One of the most popular groups of epitaphs comprise those in which the grammar of the writer has let the subject down. One favourite, variously ascribed to different places and peoples, is the following, quoted without reference in B. and H. Wedgwood, *The Wedgwood Circle*:

> Sacred to the Memory of
> Captain Anthony Wedgwood
> Accidentally shot by His Gamekeeper
> Whilst out shooting.
> 'Well done thou good and faithful servant'

Somewhat similar is an epitaph – said by Lamont-Brown to come from Cambuskenneth Abbey:

> Here lies the Body of James Robertson
> And Ruth his wife.
> 'Their warfare is accomplished'

And the much quoted epitaph from St Andrew's Church, Plymouth:

> Here lies the body of Thomas Vernon,
> The only surviving son of Admiral Vernon.

This one I am afraid I cannot trace:

> Alice Mary Johnson 1883–1947
> Let her RIP.

Nor this:

> Erected to the memory of
> John Macfarlane
> Drowned in the Waters of Leith
> By a few affectionate friends.

This piece of doggerel is persistently presented by anthologists, but again I have found no source:

> Here lies John Bun,
> Who was killed by a gun,
> His name was not Bun, but *Wood*,
> But *Wood* would not rhyme with gun,
> but Bun would.

Talking of guns, the Americans have some splendid epitaphs concerning them; this is from Sparta, California, although it is variously quoted:

> In memory ov
> John Smith, who met
> wierlent death neer this spot,
> 18 hundred 40 too. He was shot
> by his own pistill
> It was not one of the new kind
> but a old-fashioned
> brass barrel, and of such is the
> Kingdom of Heaven.

Wyndham Lewis alleges that this couplet was written by an Indian clerk on the death of Queen Victoria:

> Dust to dust, and ashes to ashes,
> Into the tomb the Great Queen dashes.

Talking of dust, there is a rather macabre epitaph on Marilyn Monroe:

> Bust to dust.
> Lashes to ashes.

Nicer certainly is the note pinned to the lectern of Nowell Myres (1902–89), Bodley's Librarian and the greatest specialist of his day in the rather obscure subject of Anglo-Saxon funerary pottery – the subject of Sir Thomas Browne's Urn Burial:

When some folk see a cemetery
The sight of it inspires
Sad memories of dust and death,
And all their lost desires;
Whilst others think of Purgatory
And everlasting fires.
But when I see a cemetery
I think of Mr Myres.

Different is the seventeenth-century poet Charles Cotton's epitaph 'on M. H.':

In this cold monument lies one,
That I knew who has lain upon,
The happier He; her sight would charm,
And touch have kept King David warm.
Lovely, as is the dawning East,
Was this marble's frozen guest;
As soft, and snowy, as that down
Adorns Blow-ball's frizzled crown;
And straight and slender as the crest,
or antlet of the one-beamed beast;
Pleasant as th' odorous month of May:
As glorious, and as light as Day.

Whom I admir'd, as soon as knew,
And now her memory pursue
With such a superstitious lust,
That I could fumble with her dust.

She all perfections had, and more,
Tempting, as if design'd a whore,
For so she was; and since there are
Such, I would wish them all as fair.

Pretty she was, and young, and wise,
And in her calling so precise,
That industry had made her prove
The sucking school-mistress of love:
And Death, ambitious to become
Her pupil, left his ghastly home,
And seeing how we us'd her here,
The raw-boned rascal ravisht her.

Who pretty Soul, resign'd her breath,
To seek new lechery in Death.

In the same sense of charity it is worth quoting, dressed in modern spelling, the lines of Thomas Kendall, published in 1577, 'On the grave of a beggar':

> While as I lived no house I had,
>   Now dead I have a grave.
> In life I lived in loathsome lack,
>   Now dead I nothing crave.
> In life I lived an exile poor,
>   Now death brings rest to me.
> In life poor naked soul unclad,
>   Now clad in clods ye be.

H. Jacob had little charity for this lady of easy virtue;

> Here Delia's buried at fourscore;
> When young, a lewd, rapacious Whore,
> Vain, and expensive; but when old,
> A pious, sordid, drunken Scold.

Washington in the summer of 1868 was cruelly hot. Anthony Trollope – not normally thought of as a versifier – was staying with Senator Sumner and wrote this punning quatrain:

> Washington has slain this man,
> By politics and heat together,
> Sumner alone he might have stood,
> But not the summer weather.

Robert Southey was made Poet Laureate in 1813 and in 1821 published an apotheosis of George III in English hexameters. This attracted the poetic ire of Byron – but he was further pilloried by Thomas Moore:

> Beneath these poppies buried deep,
>   The bones of Bob the bard lie hid;
> Peace to his manes; and may he sleep
>   As soundly as his readers did.
>
> Through every sort of verse meandering,
>   Bob went without a hitch or fall,
> Through epic, Sapphic, Alexandrine,
>   To verse that was no verse at all.
>
> Till fiction having done enough,
>   To make a bard at last absurd,
> And give his readers quantum suff.,
>   He took to praising George the Third.

And now, in virtue of his crown,
    Dooms us, poor Whigs, at once to slaughter;
Like Donellan of bad renown,
    Poisoning us all with laurel-water.

And yet at times some awful qualms he
    Felt about leaving honour's track;
And though he's got a butt of Malmsey,
    It may not save him from a sack.

Death, weary of so dull a writer,
    Put to his books a finis thus.
Oh! may the earth on him lie lighter
    Than did his quartos upon us.

John Gay was one of many poets who composed their own epitaph:

Life is a jest, and all things show it;
I thought so once, and now I know it.

Alexander Pope contributed this for him:

Well then poor G[ay] lies under ground!
So there's an end to honest Jack.
So little justice here he found,
'Tis ten to one he'll ne'er come back.

Pope is also the author of one of the very best rejected epitaphs, that for Isaac Newton; introduced by a passage in Latin is the famous couplet:

Nature and Nature's Laws lay hid in Night:
God said, 'Let Newton be!' and all was Light.

This of course led to J. C. Squire's now almost equally famous couplet:

It did not last: the Devil howling 'Ho!
Let Einstein be!' restored the status quo.

Jacob Epstein attracted the following epitaph:

From life's grim nightmare he is now released
Who saw in every face the lurking beast.
'A loss to Art', say friends both proud and loyal,
'A loss', say others, 'to the Cafe Royal'.

Oliver Goldsmith did rather better for Sir Joshua Reynolds; this epitaph is one of a number written concerning his friends, most of whom were still alive when the verses were discovered on his death:

Here Reynolds is laid and, to tell you my mind,
He has not left a better or wiser behind:
His pencil was striking, restless and grand;
His manners were gentle, complying and bland;
Still born to improve us in every part,
His pencil our faces, his manners our heart;
To coxcombs averse, yet most civilly steering,
When they judged without skill he was still hard of hearing;

When they talked of their Raphaels, Correggios and stuff,
He shifted his trumpet and only took snuff.

Modern poets too have enjoyed the epitaph as a verse form, as W. H. Auden:

The Unknown Citizen
(To JS 07/M378)
This Marble Monument
Is Erected by the State

He was found by the Bureau of Statistics to be
One against whom there was no official complaint,
And all the reports on his conduct agree
That, in every modern sense of an old-fashioned word, he was a saint,
For in everything he did he served the Greater Community.
Except for the War till the day he retired
He worked in a factory and never got fired,
But satisfied his employers, Fudge Motors Inc.
Yet he wasn't a scab or odd in his views,
For his Union reports that he paid his dues,
(Our report on his Union shows it was sound)
And our Social Psychology workers found
That he was popular in his work and liked a drink.
The Press are convinced that he bought a paper every day
And that his reactions to advertisements were normal in every way.
Policies taken out in his name prove that he was insured,
And his Health-card shows that he was once in hospital but left it cured.
Both Producers Research and High Grade Living declare
He was fully sensible to advantages of the Instalment Plan
And had everything necessary to the Modern Man,
A phonograph, a radio, a car and a frigidaire.

Our researchers into Public Opinion are content
That he held the proper opinions for the time of year;
When there was peace, he was for peace; when there was a war, he went.
He was married, and added five children to the population,
Which our Eugenist says was the right number for a parent of his generation,
And our teachers report that he never interfered with their education.
Was he free? Was he happy? The question is absurd:
Had anything been wrong, we should certainly have heard.

Martin Fagg, in *The New Statesman*, wrote this elegy on the anthologist's favourite poet, Thomas Hood:

> O spare a thought for poor Tom Hood,
> Who dazed by death here lies;
> His days abridged, he sighs across
> The Bridge of Utmost Size.
>
> His penchant was for punning rhymes
> (Some lengthy, others – shorties);
> But though his forte was his life,
> He died within his forties.
>
> The Muses cried: 'To you we give
> The crown of rhymster's bay, Thos'.
> Thos mused and thought that it might pay
> To ladle out the pay-thos.
>
> He spun the gold yet tangled yarn
> Of sad Miss Kilmansegg;
> And told how destiny contrived
> To take her down a peg.
>
> But now the weary toils of death
> Have closed his rhyming toil,
> And charged this very vital spark
> To jump his mortal coil.

An epitaph which would have been approved by Tom Hood, which in fact may well borrow from him, is this:

> Here lies one FOOTE, whose death may thousands save,
> For death has now one FOOTE within the grave.

Robert Graves wrote a rather clever epitaph, 'on an unfortunate artist':

> He found a formula for drawing comic rabbits:
> This formula for drawing comic rabbits paid,
> So in the end he could not change the tragic habits
> This formula for drawing comic rabbits made.

The Americans are masters of the 'might-have-been' epitaph:

> Mary Ann has gone to rest,
> Safe at last on Abraham's breast,
> Which may be nuts for Mary Ann
> But is certainly rough on Abraham.

Another, quoted by Shushan, concerns Brigham Young:

> Born
> on this spot
> 1802
> A Man of much Courage
> and superb
> Equipment.

It is a pity that Ogden Nash did not write more epitaphs; one (published in 1942) demonstrates his potential:

> Beneath this slab
> John Brown is stowed;
> He watched the ads,
> And not the road.

Which is certainly more elegant than this anonymous English rhyme on a similar subject:

> He passed the bobby without any fuss,
> And he passed the cart of hay,
> He tried to pass a swerving bus,
> And then he passed away.

Another modern way of death is described by an anonymous versifier:

> Here lies the body of Mary Chowder,
> She burst while drinking a Seidlitz Powder;
> She couldn't wait till it effervesced,
> So now she's gone to eternal rest

But perhaps Beachcomber (J. B. Morton) should have the last word with that most splendid of all epitaphs:

Here in a grave, remote and quiet,
Starved by a new 'reducing diet',
Lies foolish little Mrs Skinner,
Who smiled to see herself grow thinner;
And kindly death, when she had gone,
Reduced her to a skeleton.

Final page, 'Finis coronat' (the end crowns the work).
From Jacob Cats's autobiographical poem *An Eighty-Two-Year-Long Life*,
published by Jan van der Deyster, Leyden, 1732.

SOURCES

This is by no means a complete bibliography, but is intended to lead the reader to useful anthologies of epitaphs.

AMIS, Kingsley *The New Oxford Book of Light Verse*, Oxford 1978.

ANDREWS, W. *Curious epitaphs collected from the graveyards of Great Britain and Ireland*, London n.d.

ANON. *Epitaphs Grave and Gay . . . by an idle fellow in spare moments*, n.d.

BOWDEN, J. *The Epitaph-Writer . . .* , Chester 1791.

DART, J. *Westmonasterium or the History and Antiquities of the Abbey Church of St Peter Westminster*, London 1723(?).

ENRIGHT, D. J. *The Oxford Book of Death*, Oxford 1983.

HACKETT, J. *Select and Remarkable Epitaphs*, London 1757.

HOLLOWAY, J. *The Oxford Book of Local Verses*, Oxford 1987.

LAMONT-BROWN, R. *A Book of Epitaphs*, Newton Abbot 1967.

LAMONT-BROWN, R. *Scottish Epitaphs*, Gloucester 1977 .

LAMONT-BROWN, R. *Irish Grave Humour*, Dublin 1987.

LE NEVE, J. *Monumenta Anglicana 1650–1718*, London 1718.

LEWIS, D. B. Wyndham, and TREE, C. *The Stuffed Owl*, enlarged edn, London 1930.

LINDLEY, K. *Of Graves and Epitaphs*, London 1965.

ORCHARD, R. *A new selection of epitaphs and ancient memorial inscriptions*, London 1827.

PETTIGREW, T. J. *Chronicles of the Tombs, A select collection of epitaphs . . .* , London 1878.

RAVENSHAW, T. F. *Antiente Epitaphs*, London 1878.

SAFFORD, S. D. *Quaint Epitaphs*, Boston (Mass.) 1898.

SILCOCK, A. *Verse and Worse*, London 1952.

SHUSHAN, E. R. *Grave Matters*, New York 1990.

SNOW, J. *Lyra Memorialis. Original epitaphs and Churchyard thoughts in verse*, London 1847.

SPIEGL, F. *A Small Book of Grave Humour*, London 1971.

WEBB, T. *A new select Collection of Epitaphs . . .* , London 1775.

WEEVER, J. *Ancient Funeral Monuments*, London 1631 (reprinted at various dates).

INDEX